CUET

(UG) & Integrated PG

2022

Business Studies

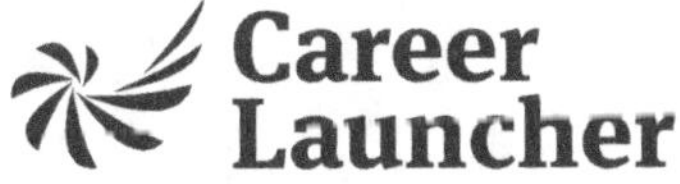

Career Launcher

Title   : CUET 2022 : Business Studies

Language   : English

Editor's Name : Akshika Gupta

Copyright ©   : 2022 CLIP

Typeset & Published by :

Career Launcher Infrastructure (P) Ltd.

A-45, Mohan Cooperative Industrial Area, Near Mohan Estate Metro Station, New Delhi - 110044

Marketed by :

G.K. Publications (P) Ltd.

Plot No. 9A, Sector-27A, Mathura Road, Faridabad, Haryana-121003

ISBN   **: 978-93-95101-21-9**

For product information :

Visit ***www.gkpublications.com*** or email to ***gkp@gkpublications.com***

CONTENTS

About CUET

A year ago, it would have been unimaginable that cut-offs in Delhi University would skyrocket to 100% for some of the undergraduate courses! While DU has always been known for its high cut-offs, there are several other universities where the story is no different.

However, the National Education Policy 2020 (NEP) aims to do away with the tyranny of the ever-rising cut-offs by introducing a Common Entrance Test for all the Central Universities in the country. NEP not only proposes a holistic approach in evaluating the students by giving them the option to select subjects based on their interest, but it also aims to simplify the process of admission to higher-education institutes.

To start with, there would be a Common Entrance Test for all the Central Universities, which would be conducted twice a year from 2022. While this might sound like a new concept to many, the fact is, there is already a CUET, which is conducted for the Central Universities established in or after 2009. As many as 14 of them already admit students based on their performance in the entrance test. The CUET scores are also accepted by four state universities of the country.

The proposed CUET aims to assess conceptual understanding and application of knowledge; and also, to lessen the burden of appearing in multiple tests.

CUET Eligibility

Getting into a premier University is every student's dream. The brand value of the University not only facilitates securing a seat in a master's program in a national/international institute, but also helps in getting job offers through campus placements.

Entry to a Central University, in most cases earlier, was based on merit, i.e., marks secured in Class XII Board exams. However, from the academic year 2021, all Central Universities will also consider the CUET score for admissions into their Undergraduate programs.

CUET 2022: Eligibility Criteria

While the official criteria will be learnt once the CUET 2021 notification is released, the stipulations are not expected to change much from those of previous years.

- A candidate must have passed Class XII (10+2) or equivalent from a recognized education Board.
- If the respective Board awards grades (or CGPA), the conversion factor given by the Board must be used to compute the percentage of marks.
- Candidates, who have completed their Class XII in 2021, and have passed the Board exams, will also be eligible to apply for CUET 2022.

Eligibility: Class XII Students

While CUET is for students who have passed the Class XII (or equivalent) Board exams, any student who is appearing for the Class XII Board exam in 2022 is also eligible to apply for CUET 2021. The candidate would be required to produce the marksheets and relevant certificates as mandated by the participating Central University, and follow the timelines provided for admissions.

Key Points

- Each participating Central University is free to decide its own eligibility criteria for admissions.

- The weightages for CUET and Class XII Board exam results(if, applicable) will be at the sole discretion of the Central University, to which admission is being sought.

- As of date, CUET does not have an age limit. However, Central Universities can fix minimum & maximum age limit for admissions to all (or any) of the programs on offer.

Reservation of Seats

As CUET is an entrance exam for admissions to Undergraduate courses at the Central Universities, which have been established under an Act of the Parliament, each Central University must follow the norms set by the Government of India, with respect to intake and reservation of seats.

Generally, the following break-up is followed:

Category	Reservation
Scheduled Castes	15%
Scheduled Tribes	7.5%
Other Backward Classes (Non-Creamy)	27%
Persons with Disability	5%

Some institutions might even have provisions for the Economically Weaker Sections, which can account for 10% of the total seats. These EWS seats are carved out from the Open Category.

To avail of the reservation benefit based on caste (or any other category as specified), a candidate must be able to produce valid documents/certificates to support such claims.

Conclusion

It is essential for every candidate to check the validity of their candidature for CUET, as well as the Central University he/she is applying to. The candidate should be aware of the documents that might be required while applying for the exam, or during the admissions.

CUET 2022 notification is expected in March 2022, and registration is also going to start then.

CUET: Exam Pattern

Examination Structure for CUET (UG) -2022:

CUET (UG) –2022 will consist of the following 4 Sections:

 Section IA –13 Languages

 Section IB –19 Languages

 Section II –27 Domain specific Subjects

 Section III –General Test

Choosing options from each Section is not mandatory. Choices should match the requirements of the desired University.

Broad features of CUET (UG) -2022 are as follows:

Section	Subjects/ Tests	Questions to be Attempted	Question Type	Duration
Section IA – Languages	There are 13* different languages. Any of these languages may be chosen.	40 questions to be attempted out of 50 in each language	Language to be tested through Reading Comprehension (based on different types of passages–Factual, Literary and Narrative, [Literary Aptitude and Vocabulary]	45 Minutes for each language
Section IB – Languages	There are 19** Languages. Any other language apart from those offered in Section I A may be chosen.			
Section II - Domain	There are 27*** Domains specific subjects being offered under this Section. A candidate may choose a maximum of Six (06) Domains as desired by the applicable University/Universities.	40 Questions to be attempted out of 50	• Input text can be used for MCQ Based Questions • MCQs based on NCERT Class XII syllabus only	
Section III- General Test	For any such undergraduate programme/ programmes being offered by Universities where a General Test is being used for admission.	60 Questions to be attempted out of 75	• Input text can be used for MCQ Based Questions • General Knowledge, Current Affairs, General Mental Ability, Numerical Ability, Quantitative Reasoning (Simple application of basic mathematical concepts arithmetic/algebra geometry/mensuration/s tat taught till Grade 8), Logical and Analytical Reasoning	

* **Languages (13):** Tamil, Telugu, Kannada, Malayalam, Marathi, Gujarati, Odiya, Bengali, Assamese, Punjabi, English, Hindi and Urdu

** **Languages (19):** *French, Spanish, German, Nepali, Persian, Italian, Arabic, Sindhi, Kashmiri, Konkani, Bodo, Dogri, Maithili, Manipuri, Santhali, Tibetan, Japanese, Russian, Chinese.*

*** **Domain Specific Subjects (27):** 1. Accountancy/ Book Keeping 2. Biology/ Biological Studies/ Biotechnology/Biochemistry 3. Business Studies 4. Chemistry 5. Computer Science/ Informatics Practices 6. Economics/ Business Economics 7. Engineering Graphics 8.Entrepreneurship 9. Geography/Geology 10. History 11. Home Science 12.Knowledge Tradition and Practices of India 13. Legal Studies 14. Environmental Science 15. Mathematics 16. Physical Education/ NCC /Yoga 17.Physics 18.Political Science 19. Psychology 20. Sociology 21. Teaching Aptitude 22. Agriculture 23. Mass Media/ Mass Communication 24. Anthropology 25. Fine Arts/Visual Arts (Sculpture/ Painting)/Commercial Arts, 26. Performing Arts – (i) Dance (Kathak/ Bharatnatyam/Oddisi/ Kathakali/Kuchipudi/ Manipuri (ii) Drama- Theatre (iii) Music General (Hindustani/ Carnatic/ RabindraSangeet/ Percussion/ Non-Percussion), 27. Sanskrit *[For all Shastri (Shastri 3 years/ 4 years Honours) Equivalent to B.A./B.A. Honours courses i.e. Shastri in Veda, Paurohitya (Karmakand), Dharamshastra, Prachin Vyakarana, Navya Vyakarana, Phalit Jyotish, Siddhant Jyotish, Vastushastra, Sahitya,Puranetihas, Prakrit Bhasha,Prachin Nyaya Vaisheshik, Sankhya Yoga, Jain Darshan, Mimansa, AdvaitaVedanta, Vishihstadvaita Vedanta, Sarva Darshan, a candidate may choose Sanskrit as the Domain].*

- A Candidate can choose a maximum of **any 3 languages** from Section IA and Section IB taken together. (One of the languages chosen needs to be in lieu of Domain specific subjects)
- Section II offers 27 Subjects, out of which a candidate may choose a **maximum of 6 Subjects.**
- Section III comprises **General Test.**
- For choosing Languages (upto 3) from Section IA and IB and a maximum of 6 Subjects from Section II and General Test under Section III, the Candidate must refer to the requirements of his/her intended University.

Mode of the Test	Computer Based Test-CBT
Test Pattern	Objective type with Multiple Choice Questions
Medium	13 languages (*Tamil, Telugu, Kannada, Malayalam, Marathi, Gujarati, Odiya, Bengali, Assamese, Punjabi, English, Hindi and Urdu)*
Syllabus	**Section IA & IB:** Language to be tested through Reading Comprehension (based on different types of passages–Factual, Literary and Narrative [Literary Aptitude & Vocabulary]
	Section II : As per NCERT model syllabus as applicable to Class XII only
	Section III : General Knowledge, Current Affairs, General Mental Ability, Numerical Ability, Quantitative Reasoning (Simple application of basic mathematical concepts arithmetic/algebra geometry/mensuration/stat taught till Grade 8), Logical and Analytical Reasoning

Level of questions for CUET (UG) -2022:

All questions in various testing areas will be benchmarked at the level of Class XII only. Students having studied Class XII Board syllabus would be able to do well in CUET (UG) – 2022.

Number of attempts:

If any University permits students of previous years of class XII to take admission in the current year also, such students would also be eligible to appear in CUET (UG) – 2022.

Choice of Languages and Subjects:

Generally the languages/subjects chosen should be the ones that a student has opted in his latest Class XII Board examination. However, if any University permits any flexibility in this regards, the same can be exercised under CUET (UG) -2022 also. Candidates must carefully refer to the eligibility requirements of various Central Universities in this regard. Moreover, if the subject to be studied in the Undergraduate course is not available in the list of **27 Domain Specific Subject** being offered, the Candidate may choose the Subject closest to his choice for e.g. For Biochemistry the candidate may choose Biology.

Candidates are advised to visit the NTA CUET (UG)-2022 official website **https://cuet.samarth.ac.in/** for latest updates regarding the Examination.

CUET Syllabus

CUET Syllabus

Before you start your preparation for any entrance exam, it is important to understand the syllabus. Otherwise, your prep will be directionless, and you might be left wondering where things might have gone wrong!

With more than 1.68 lakh seats on offer for the undergraduate courses at the 54 Central Universities, CUET is one the most competitive examinations. For this very reason, while preparing for the exam, you will need to adopt a structured approach. And in doing that, understanding the syllabus is a critical step.

CUET 2022 Overview

CUET 2022 will be a Computer-Based Test (CBT), commonly referred to as an online exam. However, there is a difference between the two terms: CBT and online. In CBT, the questions are kept constant and simply presented in an online format; whereas in an Online Test, questions are stored as a bank, and the system decides which questions are to be presented to the candidate, based on a pre-defined logic.

CUET 2022 is likely to be a General Ability Test, with focus on English Language, Numerical Ability, Logical & Analytical Reasoning, along with General Awareness and Current Affairs.

CUET 2022 Syllabus

The CUET 2022 exam pattern gives a good idea about what is in store for the candidate and how one needs to prepare for the exam.

- **English Language:** The questions in this section will test one's proficiency in the language, based on comprehension passages, fundamentals of grammar, and vocabulary. In the Comprehension section, candidates will be evaluated on their understanding of a passage and its central theme, meanings of words used therein, etc. The Grammar section entails correcting grammatically incorrect sentences, filling of blanks in sentences with appropriate words, etc. Questions on synonyms & antonyms will check one's command over English vocabulary.
- **Numerical Ability:** Questions on Numerical Ability will test the candidate's knowledge of elementary mathematics. Areas like arithmetic, number system, basics of algebra, and modern maths will be central to these types of questions.
- **Logical & Analytical Reasoning:** This section tests the candidate's ability to identify patterns & logical links, and rectify illogical arguments. It can include a variety of Logical Reasoning questions, such as those on syllogisms, logical sequences, analogies, etc., along with Analytical Reasoning questions on series, directions, clocks & calendars, arrangements, and puzzles to name a few.
- **General Awareness and Current Affairs:** The General Awareness section includes static general knowledge, while questions on Current Affairs will gauge a candidate's knowledge of national & international current affairs.

CUET 2022 may or may not have a section on subject knowledge. Once the exam notification is out in March, there will be more clarity on this matter.

While there is no syllabus explicitly mentioned by CUET, the broad idea is always presented. One must look at the previous years' papers and solve the sample papers available to form a basic understanding.

About University of Delhi

University of Delhi (commonly known as DU) was established in 1922 and is one of the largest Universities in the country. With 16 faculties, 86 academic departments, 90 colleges and 540 programs on offer, Delhi University is no doubt one of the sought-after University in the country.

With 1, 96,000 students enrolled in UG programs, Delhi University is a valued university and constantly ranked among the top in the country. DU bagged 11th Rank in NIRF 2020 and ranked 6th in QS India Rankings 2020. The University has two Campuses: North and South.

DU UG Programs

Delhi University offers several programs at the undergraduate level. With more than 60 constituent colleges, the Delhi University offers many undergraduate courses.

Please refer to the table below for the important undergraduate courses offered by the DU and the intake across each program.

Program	Intake
B. A (Pass)	11249
B. A (Hons) Geography	788
B. A (Hons) Economics	2754
B. A (Hons) History	2791
B. A (Hons) Political Science	3657
B. A (Hons) Sociology	596
B. A (Hons) Psychology	670
B. A (Hons) Applied Psychology	252
B. A (Hons) Social Work	133
B. A (Hons) Philosophy	783
B. A (Hons) English	2886
B. A (Hons) Hindi	2829
B. A (Hons) Sanskrit	1407
B. A (Hons) Punjabi	214
B. A (Hons) Urdu	207
BA(Hons) French	49

Program	Intake
BA(Hons) German	49
BA(Hons) Spanish	49
BA(Hons) Italian	49
B. Com (Hons)	7953
B.Com (Pass)	7854
Program	Intake
B.Sc. (H) Biomedical Science	162
B.Sc. (H) Botany	937
B.Sc. (H) Chemistry	1487
B.Sc. (H) Computer Science	1265
B.Sc. (H) Electronics	624
B.Sc. (H) Mathematics	2428
B.Sc. (H) Physics	1659
B.Sc. (H) Zoology	944
B.Sc. Life Sciences	1515
B.Sc. Physical Science with Chemistry	703
B.Sc. Physical Science with Computer Science	553
B.Sc. Physical Science with Electronics	247
B. Sc (Hons.) Statistics	476
B. Sc. (Prog.) Applied Physical Science Industrial Chemistry	96
B.Sc. (Hons.) Home Science	900
B. Sc. (Hons.) Psychology	57
B.Sc. (H) Food Technology	179
B.Sc. (H)Instrumentation	99
B.Sc. (H) Microbiology	238
B.Sc. (H) Polymer Science	59
B.SC. Mathematical Science	224
B.SC. (Hons.) Biochemistry	146
B.SC. Industrial Chemistry	78
B.Sc. (Prog.) Physical Science	940
B.SC. (Hons.) Geology	98

DU UG Programs Eligibility:

As the University offers multiple programs and separate intake for male and female candidates, it is important to check the university official website regularly to keep oneself updated about the eligibility for each program, which can change.

DU UG Admissions:

Until 2021, Delhi University admitted students on the basis of class XII marks. From the academic year 2022, admissions to UG programs offered Delhi University will be based on CUET. CUET will be a common entrance for admissions to UG programs offered by all the Central Universities in the country.

Delhi University UG Programs Reservation:

DU being a Central University offers reservations in admissions according to central government rules.

Schedule Caste (SC): 15% of the total seats are reserved for students who belong to SC category.

Schedule Tribe (ST): 7.5% of the total seats are reserved for students belonging to ST Category.

Other Backward Classes (OBC): 27% of the total intake is reserved for students from Other Backward Classes (OBC), excluding those from creamy layer.

Economically Weaker Section (EWS): The University has reserved 10% seats for EWS category, in accordance with the directive of Ministry of Education.

Persons with Disability (PWD): 5% of the seats are reserved on horizontal basis for students from PWD category.

About BHU

Banaras Hindu University (BHU), situated in the holy city of Varanasi, was founded by Pandit Madan Mohan Malviya in cooperation with Dr. Annie Besant, in 1916 under the act of Parliament-B.H.U Act, 1915. BHU, which is a Central University, comprises of 6 Institutes, 14 Faculties, 144 academic departments, and 4 Inter-disciplinary centers, spread over 1300 acres. The University consists of 15,000 students, 1700 teachers and 8000 non-teaching staff.

BHU was ranked 3rd among the Universities in India in 2020. According to university submissions for NIRF 2021, BHU has 10, 585 students pursuing UG programs, of which 236 students are foreign nationals.

BHU UG Programs

BHU offers a host of undergraduate programs including medical and engineering. Through its various faculties, BHU offers a range of programs which caters to students learning abilities. The University along with its main campus, also offers the undergraduate courses from the following colleges: Mahila Mahavidyalaya (MMV); Arya Mahila Post Graduate College (AMPGC), Vasant Kanya Mahavidyalaya (VKM); Vasanta College for Women (VCW); DAV Post Graduate College (DAVPGC) and Rajiv Gandhi South Campus (RGSC).

Please refer to the table below for the important undergraduate courses offered by BHU and the intake across each program/campuses.

Faculty of Arts				
Course	Campus	Intake	Status	Duration
B.A (Hons) Arts	Faculty of Arts	765	Co-Ed	3 Years
	Mahila Mahavidyalaya	286	Women	3 Years
	Arya Mahila Post Graduate College	383	Women	3 Years
	Vasant Kanya Mahavidyalaya	286	Women	3 Years
	Vasanta College for Women	412	Women	3 Years
	DAV Post Graduate College	309	Co-Ed	3 Years
Faculty of Social Sciences				
Course	Campus	Intake	Status	Duration
B.A (Hons) Social Sciences [incl. B. A (Hons) Economics]	Faculty of Social Sciences	573	Co-Ed	3 Years
	Mahila Mahavidyalaya	193	Women	3 Years
	Arya Mahila Post Graduate College	383	Women	3 Years
	Vasant Kanya Mahavidyalaya	249	Women	3 Years
	Vasanta College for Women	210	Women	3 Years
	DAV Post Graduate College	326	Co-Ed	3 Years

Faculty of Commerce				
Course	Campus	Intake	Status	Duration
B. Com (Hons)	Faculty of Commerce	286	Co-Ed	3 Years
	Vasant Kanya Mahavidyalaya	96	Women	3 Years
	Arya Mahila Post Graduate College	96	Women	3 Years
	DAV Post Graduate College	227	Co-Ed	3 Years
	Rajiv Gandhi South Campus, Mirzapur	114	Co-Ed	3 Years
B. Com (Hons) Financial Markets Management	Faculty of Commerce	62	Co-Ed	3 Years
	Rajiv Gandhi South Campus, Mirzapur	62	Co-Ed	3 Years

Institute of Science				
Course	Campus	Intake	Status	Duration
B.Sc (Hons) Maths Group	Faculty of Science	573	Co-Ed	3 Years
	Mahila Mahavidyalaya	96	Women	3 Years
B.Sc (Hons) Bio Group	Faculty of Science	383	Co-Ed	3 Years
	Mahila Mahavidyalaya	193	Women	3 Years

Faculty of Visual Arts				
Course	Campus	Intake	Status	Duration
B.F.A (Bachelor of Fine Arts)	Faculty of Visual Arts	96	Co-Ed	4 Years
Faculty of Arts				
Bachelor of Vocation (Retail and Logistics Management)	Rajiv Gandhi South Campus	62	Co-Ed	3 Years
Bachelor of Vocation (Hospitality & Tourism Management)	Rajiv Gandhi South Campus	62	Co-Ed	3 Years
Bachelor of Vocation (Fashion Designing and Event Management)	Rajiv Gandhi South Campus	62	Co-Ed	3 Years
Bachelor of Vocation (Modern Office Management)	Rajiv Gandhi South Campus	62	Co-Ed	3 Years
Bachelor of Vocation (Food Processing & Management)	Rajiv Gandhi South Campus	62	Co-Ed	3 Years
Bachelor of Vocation (Medical Lab. & Technology)	Rajiv Gandhi South Campus	62	Co-Ed	3 Years

BHU UG Programs Eligibility:

Each of the courses have different eligibility for admissions. To be eligible for admissions, one must fulfil all the criteria as laid down by the respective faculties of the University.

B.A (Hons) Arts/ B.A (Hons) Social Sciences: Candidate must not be more than 22 years of age and must have passed class XII or equivalent with minimum 50% marks in aggregate.

B.A (Hons) Economics: Candidate must not be more than 22 years of age and must have passed class XII or equivalent with minimum 50% marks in aggregate along with mathematics as one of the papers.

B. Com (Hons)/B. Com (Hons) Financial Markets Management: Candidate must not be more than 22 years of age and must have passed class XII or equivalent with minimum 50% marks in aggregate with Commerce/Economics/Maths/Computer Science/Finance/Financial Markets Management as one of the subjects.

B. Sc (Hons) Maths Group: Candidate must not be more than 22 years of age and must have passed class XII or equivalent with minimum 50% marks in aggregate in the subjects Physics, Maths plus any one of the following: Chemistry, Statistics, Geology, Computer Science, Information Technology and Geography and must have passed in each of the concerned three subjects.

B. Sc (Hons) Bio Group: Candidate must not be more than 22 years of age and must have passed class XII or equivalent with minimum 50% marks in aggregate in the subjects Physics, Chemistry plus any one of the following: Biology, Geology and Geography and must have passed in each of the concerned three subjects.

B. F. A (Bachelor of Fine Arts): Candidate must not be more than 22 years of age and must have passed class XII or equivalent with minimum 50% marks in aggregate.

Bachelor of Vocation: Candidate must have passed class XII or equivalent in any stream (Science for Food Processing and Medical Lab Technology) or level 4 NSQF certificate.

BHU UG Admissions:

Until 2021, admissions to BHU UG courses were based on Undergraduate Entrance Test (UET) conducted by the University. From the academic year 2022, admissions to UG programs offered by BHU will be based on CUET, which will replace the UET. CUET will be a common entrance for admissions to UG programs offered by all the Central Universities in the country.

BHU UG Programs Reservation:

BHU being a Central University offers reservations in admissions according to central government rules.

Schedule Caste (SC): 15% of the total seats are reserved for students who belong to SC category.

Schedule Tribe (ST): 7.5% of the total seats are reserved for students belonging to ST Category.

Other Backward Classes (OBC): 27% of the total intake is reserved for students from Other Backward Classes (OBC), excluding those from creamy layer.

Economically Weaker Section (EWS): The University has reserved 10% seats for EWS category, in accordance with the directive of Ministry of Education.

Persons with Disability (PWD): 5% of the seats are reserved on horizontal basis for students from PWD category.

About JNU

Ever wondered which University, the cadets from National Defence Academy (NDA) graduate from? Yes. It is Jawaharlal Nehru University (JNU). JNU started in the year 1969, three years after the act of Parliament in 1966. With several academic centres of JNU declared "Centres of Excellence" by the University Grants Commission, JNU has been ranked No. 1 by National Assessment and Accreditation Council (NAAC). JNU has been ranked No. 2 by National Institutional Ranking Framework (NIRF) 2020 and has been awarded the Best University Award by the President of India in 2017. The European Commission has awarded the Jean Monnet Centre of Excellence for European Union Studies in India (CEEUSI) to Jawaharlal Nehru University in 2018. This is one of the highest international recognition for any European Studies programme.

JNU was the first University to start integrated five-year Master of Arts in Language Courses. JNU actively collaborates with National and International Universities for student and faculty exchange programs.

According to university submissions for NIRF 2020, JNU has 1,048 students pursuing UG programs, of which 46 are foreign nationals.

JNU UG Programs

JNU offers a limited program at the undergraduate level, unlike other universities. The focus at undergraduate has been largely on language courses. In 2018, JNU started two programs in engineering and plans to add a few more specializations in future.

Please refer to the table below for the important undergraduate courses offered by JNU and the intake across each program.

School	Program	Intake	Duration
School of Language, Literature and Cultural Studies	B. A (Hons) Pashto	19	3 Years
	B. A (Hons) Persian	39	3 Years
	B. A (Hons) Arabic	39	3 Years
	B. A (Hons) Japanese	48	3 Years
	B. A (Hons) Korean	39	3 Years
	B. A (Hons) Chinese	44	3 Years
	B. A (Hons) French	48	3 Years
	B. A (Hons) German	48	3 Years
	B. A (Hons) Russian	68	3 Years
	B. A (Hons) Spanish	39	3 Years

School of Sanskrit and Indic Studies	B. Sc - M. Sc Integrated Program in Ayurveda Biology	20	5 Years
School of Engineering	B. Tech in Computer Science and Engineering & MS/M. Tech in Social Sciences/Humanities/Science/Technology	25	5 Years
	B. Tech in Electronics and Communication Engineering & MS/M. Tech in Social Sciences/Humanities/Science/Technology	25	5 Years

JNU UG Programs Eligibility:

Each of the courses have different eligibility for admissions. To be eligible for admissions, one must fulfil all the criteria as laid down by the respective faculties of the University.

B.A (Hons) Language Courses: Candidate must not be less than 17 years of age and must have passed Senior School Certificate (10+2) or equivalent examination with minimum of 45% marks.

B. Sc - M. Sc Integrated Program in Ayurveda Biology: Candidate must not be less than 17 years of age and must have passed Senior School Certificate (10+2) or equivalent examination with minimum of 45% marks.

B. Tech-M. Tech: Based on JEE Mains

JNU UG Admissions:

Until 2021, admissions to JNU UG courses were based on JNU Entrance Examination (JNUEE) conducted by the National Testing Agency (NTA). From the academic year 2022, admissions to UG programs offered by JNU will be based on CUET, which will replace the JNUEE. CUET will be a common entrance for admissions to UG programs offered by all the Central Universities in the country.

JNU UG Programs Reservation:

JNU being a Central University offers reservations in admissions according to central government rules.

Schedule Caste (SC): 15% of the total seats are reserved for students who belong to SC category.

Schedule Tribe (ST): 7.5% of the total seats are reserved for students belonging to ST Category.

Other Backward Classes (OBC): 27% of the total intake is reserved for students from Other Backward Classes (OBC), excluding those from creamy layer. Also, Central List of Caste to be followed.

Economically Weaker Section (EWS): The University has reserved 10% seats for EWS category, in accordance with the directive of Ministry of Education.

Persons with Disability (PWD): 5% of the seats are reserved on horizontal basis for students from PWD category.

About Jamia Milia Islamia

Jamia Milia Islamia (JMI) was founded in 1920 in Aligarh and became a Central University in 1988 by the act of Parliament. Jamia in Urdu stands for University and Milia means National, making Jamia Milia Islamia a National University. Jamia Milia Islamia moved to Delhi in 1925 and shifted to its present campus in Okhla in 1935.

Jamia Milia Islamia is a NAAC accredited University with grade "A" and was placed 10th in NIRF Rankings 2020. According to submissions made by University for NIRF 2021, Jamia Milia Islamia has a total of 5,911 students pursuing undergraduate courses at the University, of which 105 are foreign nationals. The University also manage to place a total of 681 UG students with an average salary ranging 4.2 Lacs-6.0 Lacs.

JMI UG Programs

Jamia Milia Islamia (JMI) offers a host of undergraduate programs for students. Through its various faculties, JMI offers a range of programs which caters to students learning abilities.

Please refer to the table below for the important undergraduate courses offered by Jamia Milia Islamia and the intake across each program.

Faculty	Course	Intake	Duration
Faculty of Humanities and Language	B. A (Hons) English	60	3 Years
	B. A (Hons) Hindi	40	3 Years
	B. A (Hons) Mass Media-Hindi	40	3 Years
	B. A (Hons) History	60	3 Years
	Bachelor of Hotel Management (BHM)	40	3 Years
	Bachelor of Tourism and Travel Management	40	3 Years
	B. Voc (Food Production)	40	3 Years
Faculty of Social Sciences	Bachelor of Arts (B. A)	68	3 Years
	B. Com (Hons)	55	3 Years
	BBA (Bachelor of Business Administration)	44	3 Years
	B. A (Hons) Economics	53	3 Years
	B. A (Hons) Sociology	42	3 Years
	B. A (Hons) Political Science	42	3 Years
	B. A (Hons) Psychology	42	3 Years
Faculty of Natural Sciences	B. Sc (Bachelor of Science)	50	3 Years
	B. Sc Biosciences	40	3 Years
	B. Sc Biotechnology	35	3 Years
	B. Sc (Hons) Chemistry	40	3 Years
	B. A/B. Sc (Hons) Geography	60	3 Years
	B. Sc (Hons) Mathematics	45	3 Years
	B. Sc (Hons) Applied Mathematics	45	3 Years
	B. Sc (Hons) Physics	45	3 Years
Faculty of Fine Arts	Bachelor of Fine Arts (Applied Art)	30	4 Years
	Bachelor of Fine Arts (Art Education)	20	4 Years
	Bachelor of Fine Arts (Painting)	20	4 Years
	Bachelor of Fine Arts (Sculpture)	10	4 Years

JMI UG Programs Eligibility:

Each of the courses have different eligibility for admissions. To be eligible for admissions, one must fulfil all the criteria as laid down by the respective faculties of the University.

B. Com (Hons) /BBA /B. A (Hons) Economics: Candidate must have passed class XII or equivalent with a minimum of 50% marks in five subjects.

BHM/BTTM/B. Voc (Food Production): Candidate must have passed class XII or equivalent with a minimum of 45% marks in five subjects.

B. A (Hons) Mass Media/B. A (Hons) Hindi: Candidate must have passed class XII or equivalent with a minimum of 45% marks in five subjects.

B. Sc/B. Sc (Hons): Candidate must have passed class XII or equivalent with minimum 50% marks in each of the science subjects i.e. Physics, Chemistry and Mathematics and 50% marks in aggregate of best 5-subjects.

JMI UG Admissions:

Until 2021, admissions to JMI UG courses were based on Entrance Test (JMI-ET) conducted by the University. From the academic year 2022, admissions to UG programs offered by JMI will be based on CUET, which will replace the JMI-ET. CUET will be a common entrance for admissions to UG programs offered by all the Central Universities in the country.

JMI UG Programs Reservation:

JMI is a minority reservation-based University and accordingly, seats are reserved for candidates as per the norms laid down by the University.

Muslim Minority: 30% of the total seats are reserved for Muslim applicants; 10% of the total seats are reserved for women applicants who are Muslim; 10% of the total intake is for OBC-NC candidates who are Muslims.

Persons with Disability (PWD): 5% of the seats are reserved for students from PWD category.

Jamia Students: 5% seats in all Undergraduate Programs shall be filled by internal students of Jamia who have passed their qualifying examination of the concerned programme (X or XII) from Jamia Schools as regular students.

In addition, Jamia Milia Islamia has supernumerary seats for Kashmiri Migrants and students from Jammu and Kashmir.

About Aligarh Muslim University

Aligarh Muslim University also referred as AMU was established by Sir Syed Ahmad Khan in 1875. The University started as Muhammadan Anglo-Oriental College and became a University (AMU) in 1920. The university has been ranked 801–1000 in the QS World University Rankings of 2021 and 17 in India by the National Institutional Ranking Framework in 2020.

Aligarh Muslim University is institution of national importance, under the seventh schedule of the Constitution of India.

AMU UG Programs

Aligarh Muslim University offers several programs at the undergraduate level. With 7 constituent colleges, the Aligarh Muslim University offers many undergraduate courses.

Please refer to the table below for the important undergraduate courses offered by the AMU and the intake across each program.

Course	Intake	Duration
B. Sc (Hons) Home Science	30*	3 Years
B.Sc (Hons) Agriculture	40	4 Years
B. A (Hons) Arabic	20+10*	3 Years
B. A (Hons) Communicative English	15+20*	3 Years
B. A (Hons) English	40+35*	3 Years
B. A (Hons) Hindi	40+25*	3 Years
B. A (Hons) Geography	50+20*	3 Years
B. A (Hons) Linguistics	20+25*	3 Years
B. A (Hons) Persian	15+25*	3 Years
B. A (Hons) Philosophy	20+10*	3 Years
B. A (Hons) Quaranic Studies	10+10*	3 Years
B. A (Hons) Sanskrit	15+10*	3 Years
B. A (Hons) Urdu	40+50*	3 Years
Bachelor of Fine Arts	15+15*	3 Years
B. Com (Hons)	180+100*	3 Years
B. Voc Production Technology	50	3 Years
B Voc Polymer and Coating Technology	50	3 Years
B. Voc Fashion Design and Garment Technology	50	3 Years
B. A (Hons) Chinese	20	3 Years
B. A (Hons) French	20	3 Years
B. A (Hons) German	20	3 Years

B. A (Hons) Russian	20	3 Years
B. A (Hons) Spanish	20	3 Years
B. Sc (Hons) Biochemistry	30+30*	3 Years
B. Sc (Hons) Botany	60+40*	3 Years
B. Sc (Hons) Zoology	60+45*	3 Years
B. Sc (Hons) Physics	120+35*	3 Years
B. Sc (Hons) Chemistry	120+65*	3 Years
B. Sc (Hons) Mathematics	120+40*	3 Years
B. Sc (Hons) Geography	45+30*	3 Years
B. Sc (Hons) Geology	100+30*	3 Years
B. Sc (Hons) Statistics	60+30*	3 Years
B. Sc (Hons) Industrial Chemistry	20+10*	3 Years
B. Sc (Hons) Computer Applications	40+20*	3 Years

AMU UG Programs Eligibility:

As the University offers multiple programs and separate intake for male and female candidates, it is important to check the university official website regularly to keep oneself updated about the eligibility for each program, which can change.

AMU UG Admissions:

Until 2021, AMU conducted its own entrance test to admit students for the UG programs. From the academic year 2022, admissions to UG programs offered by Aligarh Muslim University will be based on CUET. CUET will be a common entrance for admissions to UG programs offered by all the Central Universities in the country.

University of Allahabad UG Programs Reservation:

Allahabad University being a Central University offers reservations in admissions according to central government rules. Kindly check the university website for further details.

BUSINESS STUDIES

CHAPTER 1

Nature and Significance of Management

Summary

Meaning/Concept of Management: Management is the process of getting things done with the aim of achieving goals effectively and efficiently.

a. **Process:** refers to the primary function like planning, organising, staffing, directing and controlling performed by the management to get things done.

b. **Effectiveness:** means completing the right task to achieve the deputed goal within the time frame.

c. **Efficiency:** means completion of task using minimum resources

Effectiveness Vs Efficiency

Effectiveness is about doing the right task, completing the assigned job on time, no matter whatever the cost.

Efficiency is about doing the job in cost effective manner i.e. getting maximum output with minimum input.

Characteristics of Management:

1. Goal Oriented Process
2. All pervasive
3. Multidimensional
4. Continuous process
5. Group activity
6. Dynamic function
7. Intangible force

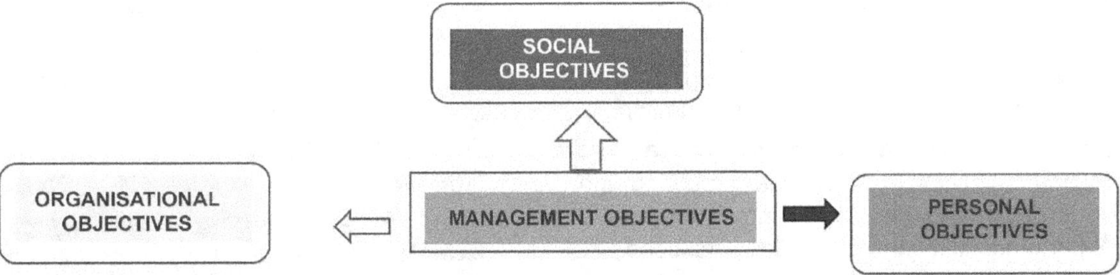

1. **Organisational Objectives:** Organisational Objectives can be divided into Survival (Earning enough revenues to cover cost); Profit (To cover cost and risk); and Growth (To improve its future prospects).

2. **Social objectives:** It involves the creation of benefit for society. As a part of society, every organisation whether it is business or non-business, has a social obligation to fulfil.

3. **Personnel objectives:** Organisations are made up of people who have different personalities, backgrounds, experiences and objectives. These vary from financial needs such as competitive salaries and perks, social needs such as peer recognition and higher level needs such as personal growth and development. Management has to reconcile personal goals with organisational objectives for harmony in the organisation.

Importance of Management

1. **Management helps in achieving group goals:** Management creates teams and coordinates with individuals to achieve individual goals along with organizational goals

2. **Increases efficiency:** Management increases efficiency by using resources in the best possible manner to reduce cost and increase productivity.

3. **Creates dynamic organization:** Management helps the employees overcome their resistance to change and adapt as per changing situation to ensure its survival, growth and its competitive edge.

4. **Achieving personal objectives:** Through motivation and leadership management helps the individuals in achieving personal goals while working towards organizational objective.

5. **Development of society:** Management helps in the development of society by producing good quality products, creating employment opportunities and adopting new technologies.

Nature of Management

1. **Management as an Art:** Art is the skillful and personal application of existing knowledge to achieve desired results:

   i. **Existence of theoretical knowledge:** Art presupposes the existence of certain theoretical knowledge.

   ii. **Personalised application:** The use of this basic knowledge varies from individual to individual.

   iii. **Based on practice and creativity:** All art is practical. Art involves the creative practice of existing theoretical knowledge.

2. **Management as Science:** Science is a systematised body of knowledge that explains certain general truths or the operation of general laws

   i. **Systematised body of knowledge:** Science is a systematic body of knowledge. Its principles are based on a cause and effect relationship.

   ii. **Principles based on experimentation:** Scientific principles are first developed through observation and then tested through repeated experimentation under controlled conditions.

   iii. **Universal validity:** Scientific principles have universal validity and application.

3. **Management as a Profession:** Profession means an occupation for which specialized knowledge and skills are required and entry is restricted.

   i. **Well-defined body of Knowledge:** is complete set of principles, concepts, terms and activities that make up a professional domain.

   ii. **Restricted Entry:** The entry in every profession is restricted through examination or through educational degree.

iii. **Professional Associations:** All professions are affiliated to a professional association, which regulates entry and frames code of conduct relating to the profession. Eg. IMA, ICAI

iv. **Ethical Code of Conduct:** All professions are bound by a code of conduct, which guides the behaviour of its members.

v. **Service Motive:** The main aim of a profession is to serve its clients.

Levels of Management

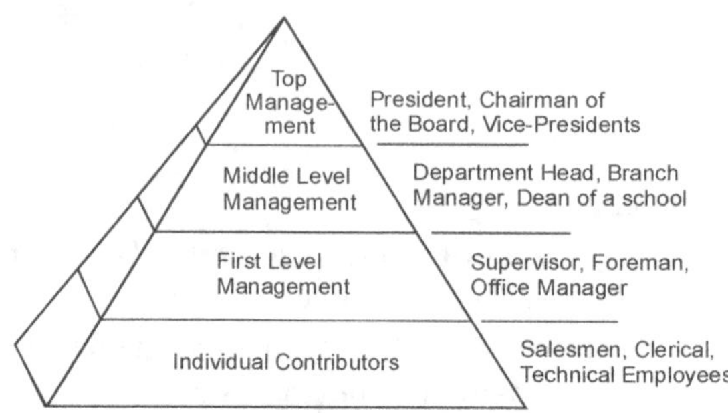

i. **Top Management:** They consist of the senior-most executives of the organisation by whatever name they are called. They are usually referred to as the chairman, the chief executive officer, chief operating officer, president and vice-president. Top management is a team consisting of managers from different functional levels, heading finance, marketing etc. These top level managers are responsible for the welfare and survival of the organisation. They analyse the business environment and its implications for the survival of the firm. They formulate overall organisational goals and strategies for their achievement. They are responsible for all the activities of the business and for its impact on society. The job of the top manager is complex and stressful, demanding long hours and commitment to the organisation

ii. **Middle Management:** is the link between top and lower level managers. They are subordinate to top managers and superior to the first line managers. They are usually known as division heads, etc. Middle management is responsible for implementing and controlling plans and strategies developed by top management

iii. **Supervisory or Operational Management:** Foremen and supervisors comprise the lower level in the hierarchy of the organisation. Supervisors directly oversee the efforts of the workforce. Their authority and responsibility is limited according to the plans drawn by the top management.

Functions of Management

Management is described as the process of planning, organising, directing and controlling the efforts of organisational members and of using organisational resources to achieve specific goals.

I.   **Planning:** Setting objectives and targets and formulating an action plan. It bridges the gap between where we are and where we want to reach.

II. **Organising:** Involves assigning duties, grouping tasks, establishing authority and responsibility relationships and allocating the resources required to perform a specific plan.

III. **Staffing:** Finding and placing the right person for the right job at the right time. It involves recruitment, selection, placement, induction and development of employees.

IV. **Directing:** Refers to leading, influencing, motivating the staff chosen to perform the assigned task efficiently and effectively.

V.   **Controlling:** Refers to monitoring organizational activities towards the attainment of organizational goals.

Coordination–The Essence of Management

Coordination is the force that binds all the other functions of management. It is the common thread that runs through all activities such as purchase, production, sales, and finance to ensure continuity in the working of the organisation.

Features of Coordination:

I.   **Coordination Integrates Group Effort:** It is an orderly arrangement of group effort to ensure that performance is at par with the plans and schedules.

II. **Coordination Ensures unity of action:** It is a binding force between various departments and ensures that all efforts are focused towards achieving the organizational goal.

III. **Coordination is a Continuous Process:** It is a never-ending process as its needs are felt at all levels and in all activities in the organisations. It begins at the planning stage and continues until controlling.

IV. **Coordination is the responsibility of all managers:** coordination is equally important at all levels of management. It is the responsibility of all the individuals in an organisation to carry out their work in a responsible manner and coordinate with each other to achieve organizational goals.

V.   **Coordination is a deliberate function:** A manager has to coordinate the efforts of different people in a conscious and deliberate manner. In other words, coordination is never established by itself rather it is a conscious effort on the part of every manager.

Exercise

1. _________ is a very popular term and has been used extensively for all types of activities and mainly for taking charge of different activities in any enterprise.
   (a) Efficiency   (b) Management
   (c) Effectiveness   (d) Objectives

2. _________ are the objectives that involves the creation of benefit for society.
   (a) Primary   (b) Secondary
   (c) Social   (d) Legal

3. _________ is the skilful and personal application of existing knowledge to achieve desired results. It can be acquired through study, observation and experience.
   (a) Profession   (b) Management
   (c) Art   (d) Knowledge

4. Management contains a series of interrelated functions that include
   (a) Planning   (b) Organising
   (c) Directing   (d) All of the above

5. _________ means the primary activities that management performs to get things done.
   (a) Process   (b) Concept
   (c) Planning   (d) Activities

6. _________ is the primary function of the management.
   (a) Controlling   (b) Staffing
   (c) Planning   (d) Directing

7. _________ is the process of doing the task correctly and with minimum cost.
   (a) Efficiency   (b) Effectively
   (c) Management   (d) Relationship

8. _________ is /are the objectives of the management.
   (a) Organisational   (b) Social
   (c) Personnel   (d) All of the above

9. **Assertion (A):** Efficiency results at performing tasks with the least wastage of time.

   Reasoning (R): It is all about doing the job in a cost-effective manner

   Codes :

   (a) Both Assertion (A) and Reason (R) are true and Reason (R) is the correct explanation of Assertion (A).

   (b) Both Assertion (A) and Reason (R) are true and Reason (R) is not the correct explanation of Assertion (A)

   (c) Assertion (A) is true but Reason (R) is False

   (d) Assertion (A) is False but Reason (R) is True.

10. A _________ motivates and leads his team in such a manner that individual members are able to achieve personal goals while contributing to the overall organisational objective.
    (a) Personnel   (b) Manager
    (c) Peer   (d) Customer

11. _________ is a systematised body of knowledge that explains certain general truths or the operation of general laws.
    (a) Art   (b) Principles
    (c) Science   (d) Profession

12. Aman has recently joined ABC Ltd, a company manufacturing Air conditioners . He found that his department was under-staffed and other departments were not cooperating with his deparment for smooth functioning of the organisation. Therefore, he ensured that his department has the required number of employees and its cooperation with other deparments is improved. Idenfity the level at which Aman was working.
    (a) Middle level   (b) Top level
    (c) Lower level   (d) None of the above

13. _________ is not the characteristics of management as a profession.
    (a) Well-defined body of knowledge
    (b) Ethical code of conduct
    (c) Service motive
    (d) Universal validity

14. Which of the following statements is not relevant to the concept of "Management as an inexact science"?
    (a) The principles of management lack universal validity
    (b) The principles of management lack universal applicability
    (c) The principles of management have to be modified according to the given situation
    (d) all of the above

15. _________ implies setting goals in advance and developing a way of achieving them efficiently and effectively.
    (a) Organising   (b) Planning
    (c) Staffing   (d) Controlling

16. Division heads and production managers can be categorised under _________ management.
    (a) Top-Level   (b) Middle-Level
    (c) Supervisory level   (d) None of the above

17. _______________ involves leading, influencing and motivating employees to perform the tasks assigned to them.

(a) Planning   (b) Staffing

(c) Directing   (d) Organising

18. _______________ is the force that binds all the other functions of management.

(a) Staffing   (b) Effectiveness

(c) Efficiency   (d) Coordination

19. Which of the following is/are the characteristics of coordination

(a) Integrates group efforts

(b) Ensures unity of action

(c) Pervasive function

(d) All of the above

20. Organisational objective is not concerned with _______________

(a) Benefit of society   (b) Growth

(c) Survival   (d) Profit

Topic Test – I

1. _______________ should be simple and clearly stated.

(a) Coordination   (b) Goals

(c) Actions   (d) Needs

2. Which of the following is not the dimension of management

(a) Management of work

(b) Management of people

(c) Management of operations

(d) Management of group

3. **Assertion (A):** Management is called an exact science.

Reasoning (R): Management deals with complex human behaviour which cannot be determined with accuracy

Codes :

(a) Both Assertion (A) and Reason (R) are true and Reason (R) is the correct explanation of Assertion (A).

(b) Both Assertion (A) and Reason (R) are true and Reason (R) is not the correct explanation of Assertion (A)

(c) Assertion (A) is true but Reason (R) is False

(d) Assertion (A) is False but Reason (R) is True.

4. In order to survive, an organisation must earn enough revenues to cover _______________

(a) Loss   (b) Goals

(c) Costs   (d) Profit

5. The main task of this level of management is to determine the overall organisational objectives and strategies for their realisation.

(a) Operational management

(b) Middle level management

(c) First line managers

(d) Top level management

6. Growth of a business can be measured in terms of _______________

(a) Sale volume

(b) Number of products

(c) Increase in the capital investment

(d) All of the above

7. Management has to reconcile _______________ with organisational objectives for harmony in the organisation

(a) Personal goals   (b) Objectives

(c) Efficiency   (d) Needs

8. The aim of a manager is to reduce costs and increase _______________ through better planning, organising, directing, staffing and controlling the activities of the organisation

(a) Efficiency   (b) Productivity

(c) Amenities   (d) Values

9. Rahul's brother is working as a section in-charge in a government office. Identify the level of management at which he is working?

(a) Middle level   (b) Lower level

(c) Top level   (d) None of the above

10. The primary reason for coordination is that departments and individuals in the organisation are _______________

(a) Dependent   (b) Interdependent

(c) Coordinated   (d) Harmonised

Topic Test – II

1. A manager has to coordinate the efforts of different people in a conscious and _______________ manner

(a) Effective   (b) Deliberate

(c) Dependent   (d) Specialised

2. Coordination begins at the planning stage and continues till begins at the planning stage and continues till _______________ .

(a) Staffing   (b) Organising

(c) Controlling   (d) None of these

3. Match the column and choose the correct answer:-

I. Effectiveness   A. doing the task correctly and with minimum cost.

II. Efficiency   B. activities that management performs to get things done

III. Process   C. doing the right task, completing activities and achieving goals.

Choose the correct option:

(a) III-A, II-B, I-C   (b) II-A, I-C, III-B

(c) I-B, II-A, III-C   (d) I-A, II-B, III-C

4. _____________ workers means simply creating an environment that makes them want to work.

(a) Leading   (b) Motivating

(c) Controlling   (d) Organising

5. Assertion (A): Management is an intangible force.

Reasoning (R): It has to adapt itself to its changing external environment

Codes :

(a) Both Assertion (A) and Reason (R) are true and Reason (R) is the correct explanation of Assertion (A).

(b) Both Assertion (A) and Reason (R) are true and Reason (R) is not the correct explanation of Assertion (A)

(c) Assertion (A) is true but Reason (R) is False

(d) Assertion (A) is False but Reason (R) is True.

6. Successful management ensures that

(a) Goals are achieved with least cost

(b) Timely achievement of goals

(c) Both of the above

(d) None of the above

7. Management is not _____________

(a) An art

(b) Profession

(c) Both art and science

(d) Pure science

8. Lola is working as a marketing manager in a company. Has been given the task of selling 50,000 units of a product and the cost of '90 per unit within 15 days. she is able to sell all the units within the stipulated time but had to sell last 200 units at 10% discount in order to complete the target. In such situation she will be considered

(a) An effective manager

(b) An efficient manager

(c) Both (a) and (b)   (d) Coordinated

9. Economic objective of an organisation includes

(a) Growth   (b) Survival

(c) Profit   (d) All of the above

10. Akarsh works as a production manager in World Fun Limited. He has been given the task of getting 1000 units of door mats manufactured at the cost of Rs. 150 per unit within 10 days. In order to be acknowledged as an effective manager, he must ensure that

(a) The cost of production does not exceed Rs. 150 per unit

(b) The work is completed within 10 days even at higher cost per unit

(c) The cost of production is less than Rs. 150 per unit

(d) All of the above

Answers

1. (b)	**2.** (c)	**3.** (c)	**4.** (d)	**5.** (a)	**6.** (c)	**7.** (a)	**8.** (d)	**9.** (a)	**10.** (b)
11. (c)	**12.** (a)	**13.** (d)	**14.** (b)	**15.** (b)	**16.** (b)	**17.** (c)	**18.** (d)	**19.** (d)	**20.** (a)

Topic – I

1. (b)	**2.** (d)	**3.** (d)	**4.** (c)	**5.** (d)	**6.** (d)	**7.** (a)	**8.** (b)	**9.** (b)	**10.** (b)

Topic – II

1. (b)	**2.** (c)	**3.** (b)	**4.** (b)	**5.** (b)	**6.** (c)	**7.** (d)	**8.** (a)	**9.** (d)	**10.** (b)

CHAPTER 2

Principles of Management

Principles of Management

A managerial principle is a broad and general guideline for decision making and behaviour. Management principles are not as rigid as principles of pure science. They deal with human behaviour and, thus, are to be applied creatively given the demands of the situation.

Nature of Principles of Management:

1. **Universal applicability:** Principles of management is applicable in all types of organizations, business as well as non-business, small as well as large enterprises depending on the nature of the organisation.

2. **General Guidelines:** They are general guidelines to action but do not provide straight solution to all managerial problems, as the business situations are complex and dynamic.

3. **Formed by practice and experimentation:** The principles of management are formed by experience and collective wisdom of managers.

4. **Flexible:** The principles of management are not rigid prescriptions, which have to be followed absolutely. They are flexible and can be modified by the manager when the situation so demands.

5. **Mainly behavioural:** Management principles aim at influencing behaviour of human beings. Therefore, principles of management are mainly behavioural in nature.

6. **Cause and effect relationships:** The principles of management are intended to establish relationship between cause and effect so that they can be used in similar situations in a large number of cases.

7. **Contingent:** The application of principles of management is contingent or dependent upon the prevailing situation at a particular point of time.

Significance of Principles of Management

The principles of management derive their significance from their utility. They provide useful insights to managerial behaviour and influence managerial practices.

(i) **Providing managers with useful insights into reality:** The principles of management provide the managers with useful insights into real world situations.

(ii) **Optimum utilization of resources and effective administration:** The resources with the company are limited. Management principles equip the managers to see the cause and effect of their decisions and actions and thus reduce wastage. Optimum utilization of resources means maximum benefit with minimum cost.

(iii) **Scientific decisions:** Decisions must be based on facts, thoughtful and justifiable in terms of intended purpose. Management principles must be timely, realistic and subject to measurement and evaluation. Principles are free from bias and prejudice.

(iv) **Meeting the changing environmental requirements:** Management principles are effective and dynamic and thus help the organization to meet the changing requirements of the environment.

(v) **Fulfilling social responsibility:** The increased awareness of the public, forces businesses especially limited companies to fulfil their social responsibilities. Management theory and management principles have also evolved in response to these demands.

(vi) **Management training, education and research:** Principles of management are at the core of management theory. As such these are used as a basis for management training, education and research.

Taylor's Scientific Management

Meaning: It implies conducting of business activities according to standardized tools, methods and trained personal in order to increase output improve its quality and reduce costs and wastes through effective and optimum utilization of resources. Hence, it stresses that there is always one best method to maximize efficiency. This method can be developed through study and analysis.

1. **Science not Rule of Thumb:** There should be scientific study and analysis of each element of a job in order to replace the old rule of thumb approach or hit and miss method. We should be constantly experimenting to develop new techniques, which make the work much simpler, easier and quicker. Scientific method involved investigation of traditional methods through work-study.

2. **Harmony Not Discord:** It means that management and workers should transform their thinking. Management should share the gains of the company, with the workers and at the same time, workers should work hard and be willing to embrace change for the good of the company.

3. **Cooperation, Not Individualism:** There should be complete cooperation between the labour and the management instead of individualism. This principle is an extension of principle of 'Harmony not discord'. Competition should be replaced by cooperation. Both should realise that they need each other

4. **Development of Each and Every Person to His or Her Greatest Efficiency and Prosperity:** It implies taking actions for the development of competencies of all persons of an organization after their scientific selection and assigning work suited to their temperament and abilities. This will increase the productivity by utilizing the skills of the workers fully.

Techniques of Scientific Management

1. **Functional Foremanship:** Functional foreman-ship is a technique in which planning and execution are separate. Functional foremanship is an extension of the principle of division of work and specialisation to the shop floor. Foremen should have intelligence, education, tact, grit, judgment, special knowledge, manual dexterity, and energy, honesty and good health. Since all these qualities could not be found in a single person so Taylor proposed eight specialists. Each specialist is to be assigned work according to her/his qualities.

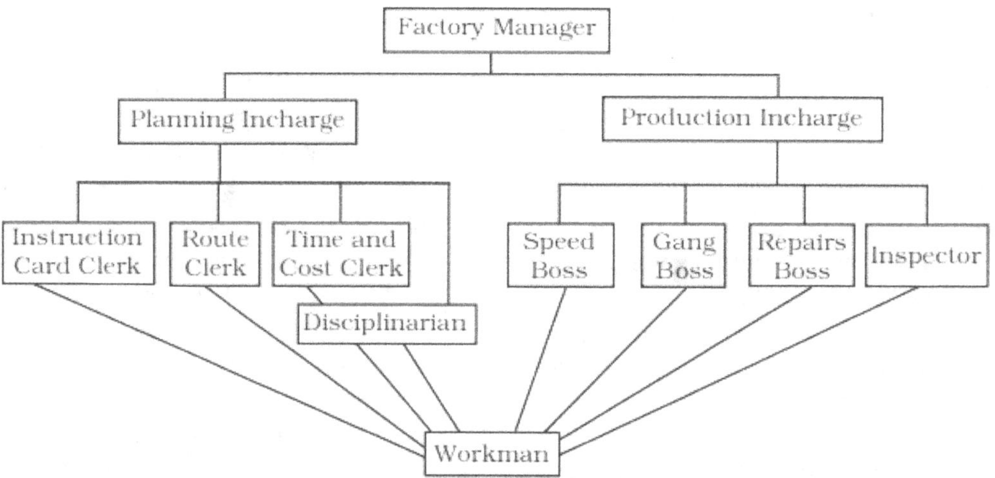

2. **Standardisation and Simplification of work:** Standardization refers to developing standards for every business activities to maximize output. Whereas simplification refers to eliminating unnecessary varieties, sizes and grades of products or services. It results in savings of cost of labour, machines and tools. It leads to fuller utilization of equipment and increase in turnover

3. **Method Study:** The objective of method study is to find out one best way of doing the job to maximize efficiency in the use of resources and to reduce cost of production and to maximizing quality and satisfaction of customers.

4. **Motion Study:** Refers to the study of productive movements. It is the science of identifying and eliminating wasteful movements resulting from unnecessary, incidental and unproductive motions of the workers so that it takes less time to complete the job efficiently.

5. **Time study:** It determines the standard time taken to perform a well-defined job. The objective of time study is to determine the number of workers to be employed, frame suitable incentive schemes & determine labour costs.

6. **Fatigue study:** Fatigue study seeks to determine time and frequency of rest intervals in completing a task. The rest interval will enable workers to regain their lost stamina thereby avoiding accidents, rejections and industrial sickness.

7. **Differential piece wage system:** This differentiates efficient and inefficient workers and links wages and productivity. The standard output per day is established and two-piece rates are used: higher for those who achieve up to and more than standard output i.e. efficient workers and lower for inefficient and slow workers. Thus, efficient workers will be rewarded & inefficient will be motivated to improve their performance.

Fayol's Principles of Management: Henri Fayol (1841-1925) was a French management theorist whose theories concerning scientific organisation of labour were widely influential in the beginning of twentieth century. According to Henri Fayol's specialization promotes efficiency of the workforce and increases productivity. In addition, the specialization of the workforce increases their accuracy and speed. There are 14 principles of management:

Principles of Management developed by Fayol:

1. **Division of work:** This principle of management is based on the theory that if workers are given a specialized task to do, they will become skillful and more efficient in it than if they had a broader range of tasks. Therefore, a process where everyone has a specialized role will be an efficient one.

2. **Authority and Responsibility:** Authority means power to take decisions and responsibility means obligation to complete the job assigned on time. There should be a balance between authority and responsibility. Mere responsibility without authority makes an executive less interested in discharging duties. Similarly, giving authority without assigning responsibility makes him arrogant and there is fear of misuse of power.

3. **Discipline:** Discipline is the obedience to organisational rules and employment agreement which are necessary for the working of the organisation. According to Fayol, discipline requires good superiors at all levels, clear and fair agreements and judicious application of penalties.

4. **Unity of Command:** According to the principle of Unity of Command, a subordinate should have only one supervisor who will be responsible for all the actions that are taken by the subordinate.

5. **Unity of Direction:** All the units of an organisation should move towards the same objectives through coordinated and focused efforts. Each group of activities having the same objective must have one head and one plan. This ensures unity of action and coordination.

6. **Subordination of Individual Interest to general interest:** The interest of an organization should take priority over the interest of any individual employee. In simple words the organisation interest to be prioritized over individual interest.

7. **Remuneration of Employees:** The overall pay and compensation should be, fair to both employees and the organization. The employees should be given fair wages so that they can have a reasonable standard of living. Wages should be within the paying capacity of the organisation.

8. **Centralization and Decentralization:** Centralization means concentration of decisions making authority with some, whereas its dispersal among more than one person is Decentralization. Both should be balanced, as no organization can be completely centralized or completely decentralized.

9. **Scalar Chain:** The formal lines of authority and communication between superiors and subordinates from the highest to the lowest ranks is known as scalar chain. This chain should not be violated but in case of emergency employees at same level can contact through Gang Plank by informing their immediate superiors.

10. **Order:** The principle of order states that 'A place for everything (everyone) and everything (everyone) in its (her/his) place'.

11. **Equity:** This principle emphasises kindliness and justice in the behaviour of managers towards workers. This will ensure loyalty and devotion

12. **Stability of Personnel:** Employee turnover should be minimized to maintain organizational efficiency. A personnel should be selected and appointed after rigorous procedure and the selected person should be kept at the post for a minimum tenure to show results.

13. **Initiative:** Workers should be encouraged to develop and carry out their plan for improvements. Initiative means taking the first step with self-motivation. It is thinking out and executing the plan.

14. **Espirit De Corps:** Management should promote team spirit, unity and harmony among employees.

Exercise

1. Principles of management are not
   - (a) Universal
   - (b) Contingent
   - (c) Flexible
   - (d) Absolute

2. Management principles aim at influencing _________ of human beings
   - (a) Behaviour
   - (b) Flexibility
   - (c) Applicability
   - (d) Tenure

3. Principles of management provide
   - (a) readymade solutions to problems.
   - (b) general guidelines.
   - (c) methods and procedures.
   - (d) rules and regulations.

4. Principles of management enable managers to learn from _________ mistakes and conserve time by solving recurring problems quickly
   - (a) Past
   - (b) Present
   - (c) Future
   - (d) None of the above

5. Management principles differ from pure science principles because management principles are
   - (a) vague
   - (b) situation-bound
   - (c) rigid
   - (d) easy to learn

6. Frederick Winslow Taylor was a _________ engineer.
   - (a) Production
   - (b) Civil
   - (c) Software
   - (d) Mechanical

7. Which one of the following is not a principle of scientific management?
   - (a) Functional foremanship
   - (b) Harmony Not discord
   - (c) Cooperation not individualism
   - (d) Science not rule of thumb

8. _________ is an extension of the Principle of Harmony not discord, there should be complete cooperation between the labour and management instead of individualism.
   - (a) Science not rule of thumb
   - (b) Method study
   - (c) Cooperation not individualism
   - (d) Fatigue study

9. _________ implies that there should be mental revolution on part of managers and workers in order to respect each other's role and eliminate any class conflict to realize organizational objectives.
   - (a) Science not rule of thumb
   - (b) Harmony Not discord
   - (c) Differential piece wage system
   - (d) None of the above

10. _________ means dividing work in small tasks/job and a trained specialist who is competent enough to perform that job does each work
    - (a) Division of work
    - (b) Centralisation
    - (c) Delegation
    - (d) Unity of command

11. _________ means power to take decisions
    - (a) Delegation
    - (b) Authority
    - (c) Responsibility
    - (d) Efficiency

12. Which principle of general management advocates that, "Employee turnover should be minimised to maintain organisational efficiency."?
    - (a) Stability of personnel
    - (b) Remuneration of employees
    - (c) Equity
    - (d) Esprit De Corps

13. According to Henri Fayol, if this principle of general management is violated, "authority is undermined, discipline is in jeopardy, order disturbed and stability threatened." Identify the principle.
    - (a) Authority and responsibility
    - (b) Discipline
    - (c) Unity of command
    - (d) Equity

14. **Assertion (A):** Motion study helps to improve the efficiency of the workers.

    Reasoning (R): It removes wasteful activitie by workers to identify the best method of work.

    Codes :
    - (a) Both Assertion (A) and Reason (R) are true and Reason (R) is the correct explanation of Assertion (A).
    - (b) Both Assertion (A) and Reason (R) are true and Reason (R) is not the correct explanation of Assertion (A)

(c) Assertion (A) is true but Reason (R) is False

(d) Assertion (A) is False but Reason (R) is True.

15. _________ is an extension of the principle of division of work and specialisation to the shop floor.

(a) Unity of command

(b) Science not rule of thumb

(c) Functional foremanship

(d) None of the above

16. Match the column:

I.	Speed Boss	A.	Keeps machine and tools prepared for work.
II.	Gang Boss	B.	Proper working conditions of machine and tools
III.	Repair Boss	C.	ensures quality of work
IV.	inspector	D.	ensures timely completion of work

Choose the correct option:

(a) I-B, II-D, III-A, IV-C (b) I-D, II-A, III-B, IV-C

(c) I-B, II-C, III-A, IV-D (d) I-D, II-C, III-B, IV-A

17. _________ refers to the study of movements like lifting, putting objects, sitting and changing positions etc., which are undertaken while doing a typical job.

(a) Motion study   (b) Method study

(c) Time study   (d) Division of work

18. _________ involves a change in the attitude of workers and management towards one another from competition to cooperation.

(a) Differential wage rate (b) Efficiency

(c) Mental revolution   (d) Time study

19. _________ is the obedience to organisational rules and employment agreement which are necessary for the working of the organisation.

(a) Agreement

(b) Penalties

(c) Discipline

(d) Unity

20. _________ means that all the units of an organisation should be moving towards the same objectives through coordinated and focussed efforts.

(a) Unity of command

(b) Centralisation

(c) Division of work

(d) Unity of direction

Topic Test – I

1. Which of the following is an objective of time study?

(a) To determine the number of workers to be employed

(b) To formulate suitable incentive schemes

(c) To calculate the labour costs

(d) All of the above

2. Mr. Anil, purchase manager of Synosis Ltd. Has to purchase 200 tons of raw material. Apart from other suppliers in the market, his brother also supplies the raw material. Mr. Anil purchases the raw material from his brother's firm at a higher rate than the market rate, which principles of management is been violated.

(a) Division of work

(b) Differential piece rate

(c) Equity

(d) Subordinating personal interest to general interest.

3. Management should find 'one best way' to perform a task. Which technique of scientific management is defined in this sentence?

(a) Time Study

(b) Method Study

(c) Fatigue Study

(d) Motion Study

4. The formal lines of authority and communication between superiors and subordinates from the highest to the lowest ranks is known as _________

(a) Gang plank

(b) Centralisation

(c) Scalar chain

(d) None of the above

5. According to Taylor, "even a small production activity like loading figures of iron into boxes can be scientifically planned and managed. This can result in tremendous savings of human energy as well as wastage of time and materials." Identify the related principle of scientific management.

(a) Harmony, not discord

(b) Science, not rule of thumb

(c) Development of each and every person to get his/her greatest efficiency and prosperity

(d) None of the above

6. Assertion (A): Principles of management are applied in a absolute manner.

Reasoning (R): Principles of management deal with unpredictable human behaviour.

Codes:

(a) Both Assertion (A) and Reason (R) are true and Reason (R) is the correct explanation of Assertion (A).

(b) Both Assertion (A) and Reason (R) are true and Reason (R) is not the correct explanation of Assertion (A).

(c) Assertion (A) is true but Reason (R) is False

(d) Assertion (A) is False but Reason (R) is true.

7. According to ________ management should promote team spirit, unity and harmony among employees.

(a) Perspective   (b) Decentralisation

(c) Division of work   (d) Espirit De Corps

8. ________ states that the overall pay and compensation should be, fair to both employees and the organization.

(a) Differential piece wage rate

(b) Division of work

(c) Remuneration of employees

(d) All of the above

9. Unity of command represents relationship between ________ and ________

(a) Superior to subordinate

(b) Organisation to organisation

(c) Activities as per organisational plans.

(d) Subordinate to superior

10. Unity of direction prevents ________ of activities.

(a) Needs

(b) Duplication

(c) Dual subordination

(d) Effective functioning

Topic Test – II

1. ________ implies that every worker should receive orders from one superior only, otherwise it will create confusion, conflict and duplication of work.

(a) Unity of command

(b) Unity of direction

(c) Division of work

(d) Centralisation

2. ________ means power to take decisions and responsibility means obligation to complete the job assigned on time.

(a) Responsibility

(b) Delegation

(c) Division

(d) Authority

3. The principles of management have been developed on the basis of

(a) Observation

(b) Experimentation

(c) Personal experiences of the manager

(d) All of the above

4. Which of the following statements best defines the techniques of management?

(a) It is a set of guidelines to take decisions and actions.

(b) It is a procedure which involves a series of steps to be taken.

(c) They are general rules for behaviour of individuals.

(d) None of the above.

5. The application of the principles of management has to be changed as per the requirements of the prevailing situation at a particular point of time. Which feature of the principles of management is being described in the given statement?

(a) Contingent

(b) Mainly behavioural

(c) Cause and effect relationship

(d) General guidelines

6. Match the column:-

	I. Instruction clerk	A. Clarifies route of production
	II. Route clerk	B. Secure discipline
	III. Time and cost clerk	C. Specifies instructions for workers
	IV. Disciplinarian	D. Creates time and cost sheet

Choose the correct option:

(a) I-D, II-B, III-A, IV-C

(b) I-A, II-C, III-B, IV-D

(c) I-C, II-A, III-D, IV-B

(d) None of the above

7. Assertion (A): Principles of management help in predicting the outcome of managerial actions.

Reasoning (R): Principles of management are based on cause and affect relationships.

Codes :

(a) Both Assertion (A) and Reason (R) are true and Reason (R) is the correct explanation of Assertion (A).

(b) Both Assertion (A) and Reason (R) are true and Reason (R) is not the correct explanation of Assertion (A).

(c) Assertion (A) is true but Reason (R) is False

(d) Assertion (A) is False but Reason (R) is true.

8. Principles of management are not

(a) Flexible   (b) Behavioural

(c) Universal   (d) Absolute

9. Gang plank is related to _______________

(a) Communication

(b) Motivation

(c) Supervision of workers

(d) Incentives of workers

10. _______________ is the technique in which each worker is supervised by eight supervisors.

(a) Unity of command

(b) Centralisation

(c) Functional foremanship

(d) Division of work

Answers

1. (d)   **2.** (a)   **3.** (b)   **4.** (a)   **5.** (b)   **6.** (d)   **7.** (a)   **8.** (b)   **9.** (b)   **10.** (a)

11. (b)   **12.** (a)   **13.** (b)   **14.** (a)   **15.** (c)   **16.** (b)   **17.** (a)   **18.** (c)   **19.** (c)   **20.** (d)

Topic – I

1. (d)   **2.** (d)   **3.** (b)   **4.** (c)   **5.** (b)   **6.** (d)   **7.** (d)   **8.** (c)   **9.** (a)   **10.** (b)

Topic – II

1. (a)   **2.** (d)   **3.** (d)   **4.** (b)   **5.** (a)   **6.** (a)   **7.** (a)   **8.** (d)   **9.** (a)   **10.** (c)

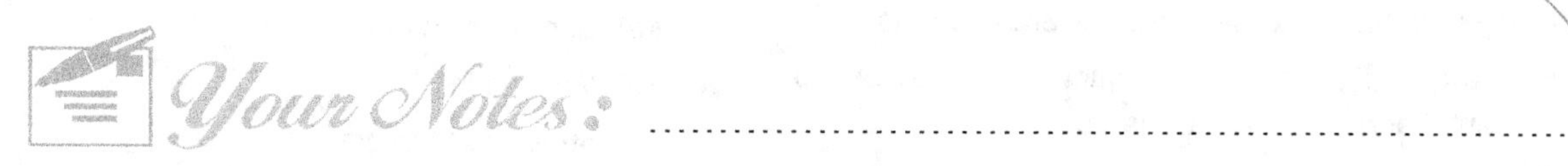

Your Notes: ....

CHAPTER 3

Business Environment

Summary

Business Environment:

Means the sum total of all individuals, institutions and other forces that are outside the control of a business enterprise but that may affect its performance.

Features of Business Environment

1. **Totality of external forces:** it includes the sum total of all external things to business firm .

2. **Specific and general forces:** Business environment includes both specific and general forces. Specific forces include investors, competitors, customers etc. who influence business firm directly while general forces include social, political, economic, legal and technological conditions, which affect a business, firm indirectly.

3. Different elements or parts of business environment are closely interrelated. For example, increased life expectancy of people and increased awareness for health care have increased the demand for many health products and services.

4. **Dynamic nature:** it is dynamic in nature as it keeps on changing in terms of technological improvement, shifts in consumer preferences or entry of new competition in the market.

5. **Uncertainty:** Business environment is largely uncertain as it is very difficult to predict future happenings, especially when environment changes are taking place too frequently as in the case of information technology or fashion industries.

6. **Complexity:** Business environment is complex phenomenon, which is easier to understand in parts, but it is difficult to understand in totality. Since the business environment consists of various interrelated and dynamic forces, it is difficult to understand the constituents of a given environment.

7. **Relativity:** Business environment is a relative concept whose impact differs from country to country, region to region and firm to firm.

Importance of Business Environment :

1. **Enables the firm to identify opportunities and getting the first mover advantage**: Environment provides numerous opportunities for business success. Early identification of opportunities helps an enterprise to be the first to exploit them instead of losing them to competitors.

2. **Helps the firm to Identify threats and early warning signal:** Environmental awareness can help managers of an organization to identify various threats on time and serve as an early warning signal.

3. **Helps in tapping useful resources:** is a source of various resources such as labour, machine, money, raw material, etc. to a business. By the concept of business environment an enterprise can design policies to acquire the required resources and convert them into output that environment desires.

4. **Helps in coping with rapid changes:** Business environment is very dynamic were changes are taking place at a fast pace. Changes such as turbulent market conditions, less brand loyalty etc. In order to cope with significant changes managers must understand, examine, and develop a suitable course of action.

5. **Helps in assisting in planning and policy formulation:** Since environment is a source of both opportunities and threats for a business enterprise, its understanding and analysis can be the basis for deciding the future course of action or training guidelines for decision making.

6. **Helps in improving performance:** The final reason for understanding business environment relates to whether or not it really makes a difference in the performance of an enterprise.

Dimensions of Business Environment

1. **Economic Environment:** Interest rates, inflation rates, changes in disposable Income of people, stock market indices and the value of rupee are some of the economic factors that can affect management

practices in a business enterprise. Short and long term interest rates significantly affect the demand for product and services.

2. **Social Environment:** Business environment includes various social forces such as customs, beliefs, literacy rate, educational levels, lifestyle, values etc. Social trends present various opportunities and threats to business enterprise.

3. **Technological Environment:** It includes forces relating to scientific improvements and innovations, which provide new ways of producing goods and services and new methods and techniques of operating business.

4. **Political Environment:** Political environment includes political conditions such as general stability and peace in the country and specific attitudes that elected government representatives hold towards business. The significance of political conditions in business success lies in the predictability of business activities under stable political conditions.

5. **Legal Environment:** It includes various laws and legislations passed by the Government, administrative orders, court judgements, decisions of various commissions and agencies at every level of the government center, state or local. Businessmen have to act according to various legislations and their knowledge is very necessary.

Economic Environment in India

In accordance with the economic planning, the government gave a lead role to the public sector for infrastructure industries whereas the private sector was broadly given the responsibility of developing consumer goods industry. At the same time, the government imposed several restrictions, regulations and controls on the working of private sector enterprises. India's experience with economic planning has delivered mixed results. In 1991 the economy faced a serious foreign exchange crisis, high government deficit and a rising trend of prices despite bumper crops.

As a part of economic reforms, the Government of India announced a new industrial policy in July 1991. The broad features of this policy were as follows:

a. Reduction in the number of industries under compulsory licensing to six.

b. The role of public sector was limited to four industries of strategic importance.

c. Disinvestment was carried out in case of many public sector enterprises.

d. Policy towards foreign capital was liberalised. The share of foreign equity participation was increased

e. Automatic permission was now granted for technology agreements with foreign companies.

f. Foreign Investment Promotion Board (FIPB) was set up to promote and channelise foreign investment in India.

Branches of New Economic Policy

1. **Liberalisation:** The economic reforms that were introduced were aimed at liberalising the Indian business and industry from all unnecessary controls and restrictions. They signalled the end of the licence-permit-quota raj.

   Liberalisation of the Indian industry has taken place with respect to:

   a. Abolishing licensing requirement in most of the industries except a short list,

   b. Freedom in deciding the scale of business activities i.e., no restrictions on expansion or contraction of business activities,

   c. Removal of restrictions on the movement of goods and services

   d. Freedom in fixing the prices of goods services

   e. Reduction in tax rates and lifting of unnecessary controls over the economy,

   f. Simplifying procedures for imports and experts.

2. **Privitisation:** The new set of economic reforms aimed at giving greater role to the private sector in the nation building process and a reduced role to the public sector. This was a reversal of the development strategy pursued so far by Indian planners. To achieve this, the government redefined the role of the public sector in the New Industrial Policy of 1991, adopted the policy of planned disinvestments of the public sector and decided to refer the loss making and sick enterprises to the Board of Industrial and Financial Reconstruction.

3. **Globalisation:** Globalisation means the integration of the various economies of the world leading towards the emergence of a cohesive global economy.

   Till 1991, the Government of India had followed a policy of strictly regulating imports in value and volume terms. These regulations were with respect to (a) licensing of imports, (b) tariff restrictions and (c) quantitative restrictions.

   A truly global economy implies a boundary less world where there is:

   a. Free flow of goods and services across nations;

   b. Free flow of capital across nations;

   c. Free flow of information and technology;

d. Free movement of people across borders;

e. A common acceptable mechanism for the settlement of disputes;

f. A global governance perspective.

Demonetisation: The Government of India, made an announcement on November 8, 2016 with profound implications for the Indian economy. The two largest denomination notes, '500 '1,000, were 'demonetised' with immediate effect, ceasing to be legal tender except for a few specified purposes such as paying utility bills. This led to eighty six per cent of the money in circulation invalid. The people of India had to deposit the invalid currency in the banks which came along with the restrictions placed on cash withdrawals. The aim of demonetisation was to curb corruption, counterfeiting the use of high denomination notes for illegal activities; and especially the accumulation of 'black money' generated by income that has not been declared to the tax authorities.

Features

1. Demonetisation is viewed as a tax administration measure. Cash holdings arising from declared income was readily deposited in banks and exchanged for new notes. But those with black money had to declare unaccounted income and pay tax penalty was imposed.

2. Demonetisation is also interpreted as a shift on the part of the government indicating that tax evasion will no longer be tolerated or accepted.

3. Demonetisation also led to tax administration channelizing savings into the formal financial system.

4. Another feature of demonetisation is to create a less-cash or cash-lite economy, i.e., channeling more savings through the formal financial system and improving tax compliance.

Impact of Government Policy Changes on Business and Industry:

(i) **Increasing competition:** As a result of changes in the rules of industrial licensing and entry of foreign firms, competition for Indian firms has increased especially in service industries like telecommunications, airlines, banking, insurance, etc. which were earlier in the public sector.

(ii) **More Demanding Customers:** Well-informed customers are more demanding. Increased competition in the market gives customer wider choice of quality products at reasonable price.

(iii) **Rapidly changing technological environment:** Increased competition forces the firms to develop new ways to survive and grow in the market. New technologies make it possible to improve machines, process, products and services. The rapidly changing technological environment creates tough challenges before smaller firms.

(iv) **Necessity for Change:** After 1991, the market forces have become turbulent, as a result of which the enterprises have to continuously modify their operations.

(v) **Need for Developing Human Resources:** The changing market conditions of today requires people with higher competence and greater commitment, hence there is a need for developing human resources.

(vi) **Market Orientation:** Earlier firms followed production oriented marketing operations. Today firms produce those goods & services as per the requirements of the customers.

(vii) **Loss of budgetary Support to the Public Sector:** The budgetary support given by the central government to the public sector had declined to a considerable extend. Thus in order to survive, the public sector have to be more efficient generate their resources and profits.

Exercise

1. Which of the following is/are the part of the business environment of business?
   - (a) Customers
   - (b) Suppliers
   - (c) Competitors
   - (d) All of the above

2. __________ the sum total of all individuals, institutions and other forces that are outside the control of a business enterprise but that may affect its performance.
   - (a) Production
   - (b) Public sector
   - (c) Business environment
   - (d) Competitors

3. Specific factors does not include__________
   - (a) Social conditions
   - (b) Investors
   - (c) Customers
   - (d) Suppliers

4. 'Christmas Wish' is a well-known resort for organising parties, especially for children. However, in past 8 months its popularity has reduced considerably as a new resort with better ambience and facilities has opened within its boundaries. Name the related feature of business environment which has influenced the business of 'Christmas wish' adversely.
   - (a) Totality of external forces
   - (b) Dynamic nature
   - (c) Interrelatedness
   - (d) Uncertainty

5. The organisation must be aware of the __________ forces.
   - (a) External
   - (b) Internal
   - (c) Social
   - (d) None of the above

6. Proper understanding of business environment is not a prerequisite for
   - (a) tapping of useful resources.
   - (b) identification of opportunities and threats.
   - (c) formulation of strategies.
   - (d) better coordination of employee efforts.

7. Business environment is a__________concept.
   - (a) Relative
   - (b) Practical
   - (c) Difficult
   - (d) Growth

8. __________refer to the positive external trends or changes that will help a firm to improve its performance.
   - (a) Threats
   - (b) Opportunities
   - (c) Efforts
   - (d) Environment

9. Which of the following is not the part of social environment?
   - (a) Monetary policy
   - (b) Customs
   - (c) Literacy rate
   - (d) Beliefs

10. Standards should be__________so that they can be changed as per the changes required.
    - (a) Rigid
    - (b) Flexible
    - (c) Static
    - (d) All of the above

11. **Assertion (A):** Business Environment is mostly uncertain.

    Reasoning (R): As it is very difficult to predict future happenings.

    Codes :
    - (a) Both Assertion (A) and Reason (R) are true and Reason (R) is the correct explanation of Assertion (A).
    - (b) Both Assertion (A) and Reason (R) are true and Reason (R) is not the correct explanation of Assertion (A).
    - (c) Assertion (A) is true but Reason (R) is False
    - (d) Assertion (A) is false but Reason (R) is True

12. Political stability builds__________among business community.
    - (a) Confidence
    - (b) Rigidity
    - (c) Flexibility
    - (d) Uncertainty

13. The entry of the multinational companies in large numbers in the Indian market has created
    - (a) Huge demand
    - (b) Huge supply
    - (c) Rigidness
    - (d) Tough competition

14. __________is the integration of world economy into a single market through removal of trade barriers between countries.
    - (a) Privatisation
    - (b) Liberalisation
    - (c) Globalisation
    - (d) All of the above

15. __________relaxed the rules and regulations which restricted the growth of the private sector and also allowed the private sector to take part in the economic activities that were exclusively reserved for the government sector.

(a) Liberalisation   (b) Globalisation

(c) Demonetisation   (d) Privatisation

16. __________means transfer of ownership of a public sector enterprise to a private enterprise.

(a) Integration   (b) Dilution

(c) Disinvestment   (d) Privatisation

17. What was the impact of demonetisation on public sector wealth

(a) High   (b) Low

(c) No effect   (d) None of the above

18. On 8th November 2016, the Government of India, ceased all the Rs.500 and Rs.1,000 banknotes. The government also announced the issuance of new Rs.500 and Rs.2,000 banknotes in exchange for the demonetised banknotes. Identify the concept being described in the above lines.

(a) Demonetisation   (b) Liberalisation

(c) Globalisation   (d) Integration

19. The Uttar Pradesh government has developed surveillance network using latest satellite technology. Under this system, the state's mining department would be in a position to check illegal mining activities across the state. The state government is also considering the use of drones in its proposed campaign against illegal mining. Identify the related dimensions of business environment.

(a) Economic dimension and Legal dimension

(b) Social dimension and Economic dimension

(c) Technological dimension and Political dimension

(d) All of the above mentioned

20. A business has to offer wider choice in purchasing enhanced quality of goods and services in order to maintain an edge over its competitors. The implementation of the new economic policy with liberalisation, privatisation and globalisation has posed various challenges for the corporate sector. One of the important challenges is explained in the above lines. Identify it.

(a) Increasing competition

(b) More demanding customers

(c) Necessity for change

(d) Market orientation

Topic Test – I

1. Which of the following is not a feature of Business environment

(a) Interrelated Elements

(b) Dynamics

(c) Complexity

(d) Continuous

2. Identification of opportunities to get first more advantage is one of the importance of business environment

(a) True

(b) False

(c) Cannot say

3. Which of the following does not explain the impact of government policy changes on business & industry

(a) Increasing competition

(b) More demanding market customers

(c) Market orientations

(d) Change in agricultural prices

4. __________refers to negative and unfavourable external factors that are likely to create hurdles for a firm:-

(a) Opportunities

(b) Warning

(c) Threats

(d) None of these

5. Which of the following are the dimensions of the business environment:

(a) Economic & Social

(b) Technological & Economic

(c) Legal & Social

(d) All of the above

6. Liberalisation means

(a) Policy of planned disinvestment

(b) Integrating among economies

(c) End of license & reduction of government control

(d) None of these

7. Globalization does not involve:

(a) Reduction of barrier

(b) Free flow of goods & services

(c) Global mechanism for settlement of economic disputes

(d) Free flow of capital

8. Which of the following are the impact of govt. policy changes on business & industry?
   (a) Increased competition
   (b) Need for change
   (c) Demanding customers
   (d) All of the above

9. Since more number of people have become more beauty and health conscious, our economy has witnessed an unprecedented surge in the number of health and beauty spas and wellness clinics. Related feature of business environment being described in the above lines is–
   (a) Totality of external forces
   (b) Dynamic nature
   (c) Interrelatedness
   (d) Relativity

10. Which one of the following is the impact of Government policy changes on business and industry?
   (a) Increase in agricultural productivity
   (b) Increase in product prices
   (c) Increase in competition
   (d) Increase in urbanisation

Topic Test – II

1. "The nature of the relationship of our country with foreign countries", is a major element of which of the following components of the Business Environment?
   (a) Social Environment
   (b) Legal Environment
   (c) Political Environment
   (d) Economic Environment

2. As part of regulations to be followed by advertisers, the advertisement for a new brand of baby products for infants provides important information for potential buyers that it is "Not recommended for infants under the age of three months". Which dimension of the business environment is highlighted in the above statement?
   (a) Social Environment
   (b) Legal Environment
   (c) Political Environment
   (d) Economic Environment

3. Atul, a bee keeper since April 2021 is now part of the growing tribe of at least 40 urban dwellers across uttar Pradesh raising bees and harvesting honey in their balconies, rooftops and back gardens. As he had been focussed on eating right the thought of domesticating honey bees to promote healthy consumption habits and seeing honey being cultivated right before his eyes was mesmerising for him. Identify the factor constituting the general environment being discussed above.
   (a) Economic environment
   (b) Social environment
   (c) Technological environment
   (d) Political environment

4. **Assertion (A):** Business environment is a complex process
   Reasoning (R): It consists of Various dynamic forces
   Codes :
   (a) Both Assertion (A) and Reason (R) are true and Reason (R) is the correct explanation of Assertion (A).
   (b) Both Assertion (A) and Reason (R) are true and Reason (R) is not the correct explanation of Assertion (A)
   (c) Assertion (A) is true but Reason (R) is False
   (d) Assertion (A) is False but Reason (R) is True.

5. Which of the following is not a component of specific forces of business environment?
   (a) Technological conditions
   (b) Customers
   (c) Employees
   (d) Investors

6. __________ refer to the external environment trends and changes that will hinder a firm's performance.
   (a) Performance
   (b) Opportunities
   (c) Threats
   (d) Adaptation

7. Liberalisation led to__________
   (a) License permit quota raj
   (b) External business
   (c) Exports
   (d) Competitive market

8. State which of the following statement is true

Statement I: Demonetisation helped to create a less-cash or cash-lite economy

Statement II: Globalisation involves an increased level of interaction and interdependence among the various nations of the global economy

Choose the correct option:

(a) I is true, II is false

(b) Both I and II are true

(c) Both I and II are false

(d) II is true, I is false

9. _________means transfer of the public sector enterprises to the private sector.

(a) Disinvestments   (b) Globalisation

(c) Privatisation   (d) None of the above

10. Match the column:

I.   Specific forces   A. social, political, legal and technological conditions

II. General forces   B. investors, customers, competitors and suppliers

III. Dynamic nature   C. shifts in consumer preference of new competition in the market.

Choose the correct option:

(a) I-B, II-C, III-A

(b) I-B, II-A, III-C

(c) I-C, II-B, III-A

(d) None of the above

Answers

1. (d)	**2.** (c)	**3.** (a)	**4.** (b)	**5.** (a)	**6.** (c)	**7.** (a)	**8.** (b)	**9.** (a)	**10.** (b)
11. (a)	**12.** (a)	**13.** (d)	**14.** (c)	**15.** (a)	**16.** (c)	**17.** (c)	**18.** (a)	**19.** (c)	**20.** (a)

Topic – I

1. (d)	**2.** (a)	**3.** (d)	**4.** (c)	**5.** (d)	**6.** (c)	**7.** (a)	**8.** (d)	**9.** (c)	**10.** (c)

Topic – II

1. (c)	**2.** (b)	**3.** (b)	**4.** (c)	**5.** (a)	**6.** (c)	**7.** (a)	**8.** (b)	**9.** (a)	**10.** (b)

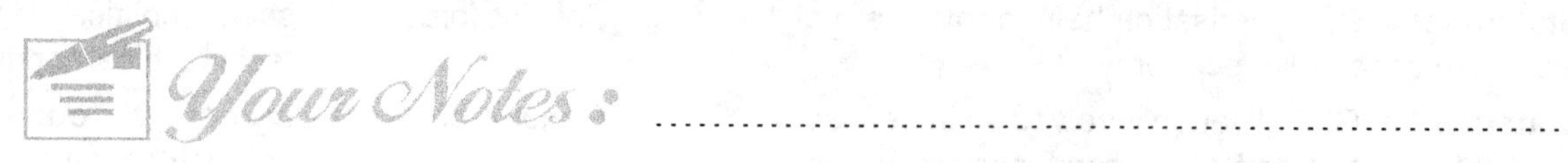
Your Notes :

CHAPTER 4

Planning

Chapter Summary

Planning is deciding in advance what to do and how to do. It is one of the basic managerial functions. It seeks to bridge seeks to bridge the gap between where we are and where we want to go. Planning is what managers at all levels do. It requires taking decisions since it involves making a choice from alternative courses of action.

It involves setting objectives and developing appropriate courses of action to achieve these objectives.

Importance of Planning :

1. **Planning provides directions:** Planning provides the directions to the efforts of employees. Planning makes clear what employees have to do, how to do etc.

2. **Planning reduces the risks of uncertainity:** Helps manager to look ahead and anticipate the changes. The plans are made to overcome the uncertainties.

3. **Planning reduces overlapping and wasteful activities:** Planning serves as the basis of coordinating the activities and efforts of different divisions, departments and individuals. It helps in avoiding confusion and misunderstanding.

4. **Planning promotes innovative ideas:** Since planning is the first function of management, new ideas can take the shape of concrete plans.

5. **Planning facilitates decision making:** Planning helps the manager to look into the future and make a choice from amongst various alternative courses of action. The manager has to evaluate each alternative and select the most viable proposition.

6. **Planning establishes standards for controlling:** Planning involves setting of goals. The entire managerial process is concerned with accomplishing predetermined goals through planning, organising, staffing, directing and controlling. Planning provides the goals or standards against which actual performance is measured.

Features of Planning

I. **Planning focuses on achieving objectives:** Organisations are set up with a general purpose in view. Specific goals are set out in the plans along with the activities to be undertaken to achieve the goals.

II. **Planning is a primary function of management:** Planning lays down the base for other functions of management.

III. **Planning is pervasive:** Planning is required at all levels of management as well as in all departments of the organisation.

IV. Planning is Continuous Planning is a never ending or continuous process because after making plans also one has to be in touch with the changes in changing environment and in the selection of one best way.

V. Planning is Futuristic Planning always means looking ahead, it is never for the past. All the managers try to make predictions and assumptions for future.

VI. **Planning is a mental exercise:** Planning requires application of the mind involving foresight, intelligent imagination and sound judgement. It is basically an intellectual activity of thinking rather than doing, because planning determines the action to be taken.

Limitations of Planning

I. **Planning Leads to Rigidity:** Once plans are made to decide the future course of action the manager may not be in a position to change them.

II. Planning May Not Work in a Dynamic Environment Business environment is very dynamic as there are continuously changes. It becomes very difficult to forecast these future changes. Plans may fail if the changes are very frequent.

III. Planning Reduces Creativity With the planning the managers of the organisation start working rigidly and they become the blind followers of the plan only.

IV. **Planning Involves Huge Costs:** When plans are drawn up huge costs are involved in their formulation. Detailed plans require scientific calculations to ascertain facts and figures.

V. **Planning is a Time Consuming Process:** Sometimes plans to be drawn up take so much of time that there is not much time left for their implementation.

VI. **Planning Doe Not Guarantee Success:** Planning only provides a base for analysing future. It is not a solution for future course of action.

Planning Process

I. **Setting Objectives:** In planning function manager begin with setting up of objectives because all the policies, procedures and methods are framed for achieving objectives only.

II. **Developing Premises:** As planning is concerned with the future which is uncertain therefore, the manger is required to make certain assumptions about the future. The premises or assumptions must be the same for all and there should be total agreement on them. All managers involved in planning should be familiar with and use the same assumptions

III. **Identifying Alternative Courses of Action:** of Action After setting up of objectives the managers make a list of alternatives through which the organisation can achieve its objectives.

IV. Evaluating Alternative Courses After making the list of various alternatives along with the assumptions supporting them the manager starts evaluating each and every alternative.

V. Selecting an Alternative The best alternative is selected but as such there is no mathematical formula to select the best alternative. Some times instead of selecting one alternative a combination of different alternatives can also be selected.

VI. Implementing the Plan This is the step where other managerial functions also come in to the picture. The step is concerned with putting the plan into action i.e., doing what is required.

VII. Follow-up Action Planning is a continuous process so the manager's job does not get over simply by putting the plan into action. The manager monitor the plan carefully while it is implemented.

Types of Plans:

Single-use Plan: A single-use plan is developed for a one-time event or project. Such a course of action is not likely to be repeated in future, i.e., they are for non-recurring situations. The duration of this plan may depend upon the type of the project. It may span a week or a month.

Standing Plan: A standing plan is used for activities that occur regularly over a period of time. It is designed to ensure that internal operations of an organisation run smoothly. Such a plan greatly enhances efficiency in routine decision-making. It is usually developed once but is modified from time to time to meet business needs as required.

Objectives: Objectives are the ends towards which the activities are directed. They are the end result of every activity, e.g., increase in sale by 10%.

Strategy: provides the broad contours of an organisation's business. It will also refer to future decisions defining the organisations direction and scope in the long run.

Policy: are general statements that guide thinking or channelise energies towards a particular direction. Policies provide a basis for interpreting strategy which is usually stated in general terms. They are guides to managerial action and decisions in the implementation of strategy.

Procedure: are routine steps on how to carry out activities. They detail the exact manner in which any work is to be performed. They are specified in a chronological order

Method: provide the prescribed ways or manner in which a task has to be performed considering the objective. It deals with a task comprising one step of a procedure and specifies how this step is to be performed.

Rule: are specific statements that inform what is to be done. They do not allow for any flexibility or discretion. It reflects a managerial decision that a certain action must or must not be taken.

Programme: are detailed statements about a project which outlines the objectives, policies, procedures, rules.

Budget: is a statement of expected results expressed in numerical terms.

Exercise

1. Planning is closely connected with creativity and
   ____
   (a) numbers   (b) statements
   (c) strategy   (d) innovation

2. Which of the following is not the importance of planning
   (a) Reduces the risk of uncertainty
   (b) Reduces overlapping and wasteful activities
   (c) Facilitates decision making
   (d) Is pervasive

3. __________ is the primary function of management.
   (a) Planning   (b) Controlling
   (c) Staffing   (d) Organising

4. **Assertion (A):** Planning bridges the gap between where we are and where we want to go
   Reasoning (R): Planning involves setting the goals and taking appropriate action to achieve these goals
   Codes :
   (a) Both Assertion (A) and Reason (R) are true and Reason (R) is the correct explanation of Assertion (A).
   (b) Both Assertion (A) and Reason (R) are true and Reason (R) is not the correct explanation of Assertion (A).
   (c) Assertion (A) is true but Reason (R) is False
   (d) Assertion (A) is False but Reason (R) is true.

5. Planning requires logical and systematic thinking rather than guess work or wishful thinking. Identify the related feature of planning.
   (a) Planning is futuristic
   (b) Planning is a mental exercise.
   (c) Planning establishes standards for controlling
   (d) Planning focuses on achieving objectives.

6. Planning cannot foresee everything and thus, there may be obstacles to effective planning. Identify the limitation of planning
   (a) Rigidity
   (b) Continuous process
   (c) May not work in dynamic environment
   (d) Reduces creativity

7. __________ is the third step in planning process
   (a) Setting objectives
   (b) Developing premises
   (c) Identifying alternative courses of action
   (d) Selecting an alternative

8. All other managerial functions are performed within the framework of the plans drawn. Identify the related feature of planning.
   (a) Planning focuses on achieving objectives.
   (b) Planning is pervasive.
   (c) Planning is futuristic.
   (d) Planning is primary function of management

9. A __________ plan is used for activities that occur regularly over a period of time. It is designed to ensure that internal operations of an organisation run smoothly.
   (a) Standing   (b) Single use
   (c) Policy   (d) Rules

10. __________ are defined as ends which the management seeks to achieve its operations.
    (a) Strategy   (b) Plans
    (c) Objectives   (d) None of the above

11. __________ refer to future decisions defining the organisations direction and scope in the long run.
    (a) Policy   (b) Strategy
    (c) Goals   (d) Objectives

12. __________ are routine steps on how to carry out activities and are specified in a chronological order.
    (a) Procedures
    (b) Single use plans
    (c) Managerial decisions
    (d) Programmes

13. __________ is a plan which quantifies future facts and figures.
    (a) Bars   (b) Budget
    (c) Method   (d) Surplus

14. A strategy is derived from
    (a) Policy   (b) Objective
    (c) Method   (d) Rule

15. **Assertion (A):** Planning provides innovative ideas
    Reasoning (R): It provides the standards against which actual performance is measured
    Codes :
    (a) Both Assertion (A) and Reason (R) are true and Reason (R) is the correct explanation of Assertion (A).
    (b) Both Assertion (A) and Reason (R) are true and Reason (R) is not the correct explanation of Assertion (A).
    (c) Assertion (A) is true but Reason (R) is False
    (d) Assertion (A) is False but Reason (R) is true.

16. Planning requires logical and systematic thinking rather than guess work or wishful thinking. Identify the related feature of planning.

(a) Is a mental exercise

(b) Is futuristic

(c) Continuous process

(d) Flexible

17. Sumit is striving to earn a profit of 25% in the current financial year. Identify the type of plan being described in the above lines.

(a) standards   (b) Method

(c) Objective   (d) policy

18. Which of the following statement is false with respect to planning

(a) Involves setting objectives

(b) Basic managerial function

(c) Does not reduce the risk of uncertainty

(d) Facilitates decision making

19. "Planning is required in all organisations at all level and all departments." Which feature of the planning states that

(a) Establishes standards

(b) Provides direction

(c) Continuous process

(d) Pervasive

20. According to a survey of 150 make up products companies by a reputedfirm, 60% of brand owners say they're going to spend significantly more on ingredients of the product as it is critical to their brand's success.

Identify the type of plan being described in the above lines.

(a) Policy   (b) Strategy

(c) Programme   (d) Objective

Topic Test – I

1. Objectives provide ___________ for all the managerial decisions and actions.

(a) Direction   (b) Strategy

(c) Plans   (d) Course

2. Viyo Ltd. devoted a lot of time and money to its plan. The limitation of planning here is ___________

(a) Time – consuming process

(b) Pervasive

(c) Involves huge cost

(d) Does not guarantee success

3. ___________ serves as the basis of coordinating the activities and efforts of different divisions, departments and individuals.

(a) Standards   (b) Planning

(c) Eliminations   (d) Controlling

4. "Planning is required at all levels of management as well as in all departments of the organisation." State the feature of the planning mentioned

(a) Focus on achieving goals

(b) Primary function

(c) Continuous process

(d) Is pervasive

5. Assertion (A) : Planning is a primary function of management

Reasoning (R) : Planning has no meaning unless it contributes to the achievement of goals

Codes :

(a) Both Assertion (A) and Reason (R) are true and Reason (R) is the correct explanation of Assertion (A).

(b) Both Assertion (A) and Reason (R) are true and Reason (R) is not the correct explanation of Assertion (A)

(c) Assertion (A) is true but Reason (R) is False

(d) Assertion (A) is False but Reason (R) is True.

6. "Planning requires logical and systematic thinking rather than guess work or wishful thinking". The feature of planning is ___________

(a) Involves decision thinking

(b) Is pervasive

(c) Is a mental exercise

(d) Is futuristic

7. Arrange the planning process in correct order:-

(a) Setting objectives, identifying courses, evaluating the courses , developing premises

(b) Developing premises, evaluating courses, identifying, setting objectives

(c) Setting objectives, developing premises, identifying, evaluating the courses

(d) None of the above

8. Once objectives are laid ___________ are made by the manager.

(a) Assumptions   (b) Alternatives

(c) Goals   (d) Rules

9. Which planning process is concerned with putting the plan into action, i.e., doing what is required.

    (a) Setting objectives

    (b) Selecting an alternative

    (c) Follow up action

    (d) Implementing the plan

10. __________ is not a part of standing plan

    (a) Policies   (b) Strategy

    (c) Methods   (d) Rules

Topic Test – II

1. __________ are usually set by the top management and serve as a guide for overall planning.

    (a) Strategy   (b) Rules

    (c) Policy   (d) Objectives

2. __________ are general statements that guide thinking or channelise energies towards a particular direction

    (a) Policy   (b) Plan

    (c) Rules   (d) Methods

3. Name the type of plan which provides the broad outline of an organisation .

    (a) Rules   (b) Strategy

    (c) Programmes   (d) Policy

4. By comparing __________ with standards manager can know whether the goals are achieved or not

    (a) Risk   (b) Ideas

    (c) Actual performance   (d) Costs

5. __________ forecasts the sales of different products in each area for particular month

    (a) Sales budget   (b) Sales accounts

    (c) Sales cost   (d) None of the above

6. The sub ordinates are given complete freedom in taking decisions is a part of

    (a) Rule   (b) Stratergy

    (c) Policy   (d) Procedure

7. Identify the correct sequence of steps involved in the planning process.

    (a) Evaluating alternative courses, Identifying alternative course of actions, Setting objectives, Developing premises

    (b) Setting objectives, Identifying alternative course of actions, Evaluating alternative courses, Developing premises

    (c) Setting objectives, Developing premises, Identifying alternative course of actions, Evaluating alternative courses

    (d) Setting objectives, Developing premises, Identifying alternative course of actions, Evaluating alternative courses.

8. __________ type of plan is not likely to be repeated in future

    (a) Standing plan   (b) Programme

    (c) Single use plan   (d) Method

9. __________ are detailed statements about a project which outlines the objectives, rules, etc.

    (a) Budget   (b) Programme

    (c) Single use plan   (d) Policy

10. **Assertion (A) :** Planning is a forward looking process

    Reasoning (R) : Managers try to predict and make assumptions for the future

    Codes :

    (a) Both Assertion (A) and Reason (R) are true and Reason (R) is the correct explanation of Assertion (A).

    (b) Both Assertion (A) and Reason (R) are true and Reason (R) is not the correct explanation of Assertion (A).

    (c) Assertion (A) is true but Reason (R) is False

    (d) Assertion (A) is False but Reason (R) is true.

Answers

1. (d)	2. (d)	3. (a)	4. (a)	5. (b)	6. (c)	7. (c)	8. (d)	9. (a)	10. (c)
11. (b)	12. (a)	13. (b)	14. (b)	15. (b)	16. (a)	17. (c)	18. (c)	19. (d)	20. (b)

Topic – I

1. (a)	2. (c)	3. (b)	4. (d)	5. (b)	6. (c)	7. (c)	8. (a)	9. (d)	10. (b)

Topic – II

1. (d)	2. (a)	3. (c)	4. (c)	5. (a)	6. (c)	7. (c)	8. (d)	9. (b)	10. (a)

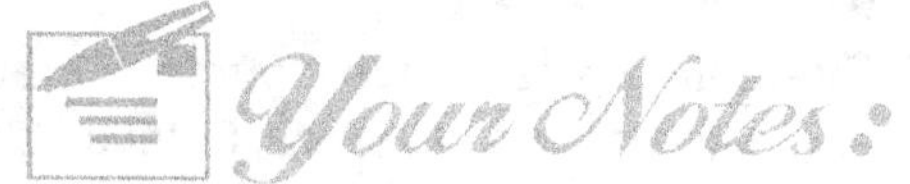 *Your Notes :* ....

CHAPTER 5

Organising

Summary

Organising can be defined as a process that initiates implementation of plans by clarifying jobs and working relationships and effectively deploying resources for attainment of identified and desired results. The aim of organizing is to enable people to work together for a common purpose.

Steps in the Process of Organising:

(i) **Identification and division of work:** The first step in the process of organising involves identifying and dividing the work that has to be done in accordance with previously determined plans.

(ii) **Departmentalization:** Once work is divided into small activities, similar and related jobs are grouped together. This grouping is called departmentalization

(iii) **Assignment of duties:** It is necessary to define the work of different job positions and accordingly allocate work to various employees. Once departments have been formed, each of them is placed under the charge of an individual.

(iv) **Establishing authority and reporting relationships:** Merely allocating work is not enough. Each individual should also know who he has to take orders from and to whom he is accountable.

Importance of Organising:

i. **Benefits of specialization:** leads to a systematic allocation of jobs amongst the work force. The division of work into smaller jobs reduces workload and enhance productivity and repetitive performance leads to specialization.

ii. **Clarity in working relationships:** The establishment of working relationships clarifies lines of communication and specifies who is to report to whom. It helps in creating a hierarchical order thereby enabling the fixation of responsibility and specification of the extent of authority to be exercised by an individual.

iii. **Optimum utilisation of resources:** Organising leads to the proper usage of all material, financial and human resources. The proper assignment of jobs avoids overlapping of work and also makes possible the best use of resources.

iv. **Adaptation to change:** The process of organising allows a business enterprise to accommodate changes in the business environment.

v. **Effective administration:** Organising provides a clear description of jobs and related duties. This helps to avoid confusion and duplication. Clarity in working relationships enables proper execution of work. Management of an enterprise thereby becomes easy and this brings effectiveness in administration.

vi. **Development of personnel:** Organising stimulates creativity amongst the managers. Effective delegation allows the managers to reduce their workload by assigning routine jobs to their subordinates.

vii. **Expansion and growth:** Organising helps in growth & diversification of an enterprise. By adding more job positions, departments, products lines, new geographical territories etc. and thus will help to increase customer base, sales and profit.

Organisation Structure: Organisation structure is the outcome of the organising process. An effective structure will result in increased profitability of the enterprise. Under the organizational structure, various posts are created to perform different activities for the attainment of the predetermined objectives of the enterprise. The structure provides a basis or framework for managers and other employees to perform their functions.

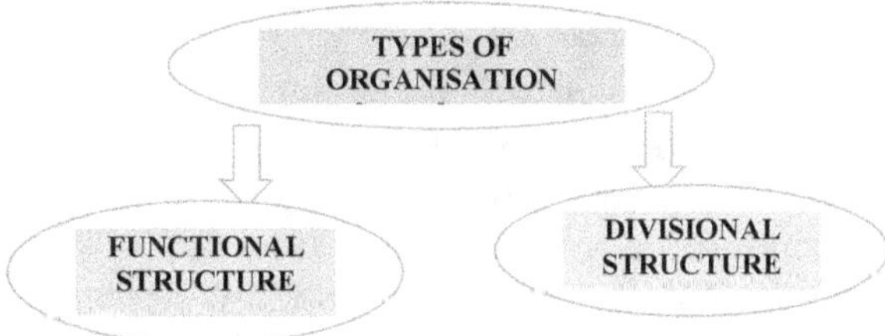

Functional structure: Grouping of jobs of similar nature under functional and organising these major functions as separate departments creates a functional structure. All departments report to a coordinating head.

Advantages:

(a) A functional structure leads to occupational specialisation since emphasis is placed on specific functions.

(b) It promotes control and coordination within a department because of similarity in the tasks being performed.

(c) It helps in increasing managerial and operational efficiency and this results in increased profit.

(d) It leads to minimal duplication of effort which results in economies of scale and this lowers cost.

(e) It makes training of employees easier as the focus is only on a limited range of skills.

(f) It ensures that different functions get due attention.

Disadvantages:

(a) A functional structure places less emphasis on overall enterprise objectives than the objectives pursued by a functional head.

(b) It may lead to problems in coordination as information has to be exchanged across functionally differentiated departments.

(c) A conflict of interests may arise when the interests of two or more departments are not compatible.

(d) It may lead to inflexibility as people with same skills and knowledge base may develop a narrow perspective

Suitability: organisations which require high degree of functional specialization with diversified activities. Large organisations producing one line of product.

Divisional Structure: In a divisional structure, the organisation structure comprises of separate business units or divisions Each unit has a divisional manager responsible for performance and who has authority over the unit.

Advantages:

(a) Product specialisation helps in the development of varied skills in a divisional head and this prepares him for higher positions.

(b) Divisional heads are accountable for profits, as revenues and costs related to different departments can be easily identified and assigned to them. This provides a proper basis for performance measurement. It also helps in fixation of responsibility in cases of poor performance of the division and appropriate remedial action can be taken.

(c) It promotes flexibility and initiative because each division functions as an autonomous unit which leads to faster decision making.

(d) It facilitates expansion and growth as new divisions can be added without interrupting the existing operations.

Disadvantages:

a. Conflict may arise among different divisions with reference to allocation of funds and further a particular division may seek to maximise its profits at the cost of other divisions.

b. It may lead to increase in costs since there may be a duplication of activities across products. Providing each division with separate set of similar functions increases expenditure.

c. It provides managers with the authority to supervise all activities related to a particular division.

Suitability: Divisional structure is suitable for those business enterprises where a large variety of products are manufactured using different productive resources.

Formal and Informal Organisation: Formal organisation refers to the organisation structure that is designed by the management to accomplish organizational goals. In a formal organisation the boundaries of authority & responsibility is clearly defined and there is a systematic coordination among the various activities to achieve organizational objectives

Advantages:

(a) It is easier to fix responsibility since mutual relationships are clearly defined.

(b) There is no ambiguity in the role that each member has to play as duties are specified. This also helps in avoiding duplication of effort.

(c) Unity of command is maintained through an established chain of command.

(d) It leads to effective accomplishment of goals by providing a framework for the operations to be performed and ensuring that each employee knows the role he has to play.

(e) It provides stability to the organisation. This is because behaviour of employees can be fairly predicted since there are specific rules to guide them.

Limitations:

(a) The formal communication may lead to procedural delays as the established chain of command has to be followed which increases the time taken for decision making.

(b) Poor organisation practices may not provide adequate recognition to creative talent, since it does not allow any deviations from rigidly laid down polices.

(c) It is difficult to understand all human relationships in an enterprise as it places more emphasis on structure and work. Hence, the formal organisation does not provide a complete picture of how an organisation works

Informal Organisation: Interaction among people at work gives rise to a 'network of social relationships among employees' called the informal organisation. The main purpose of this organization structure is the psychological satisfaction of the employees with common interests.

Advantages:

(a) Prescribed lines of communication are not followed. Thus, the informal organisation leads to faster spread of information as well as quick feedback.

(b) It helps to fulfill the social needs of the members and allows them to find like minded people. This enhances their job satisfaction since it gives them a sense of belongingness in the organisation.

(c) It contributes towards fulfillment of organisational objectives by compensating for inadequacies in the formal organisation.

Delegation: "Delegation of authority merely means the granting of authority to subordinates to operate within prescribed limits."

Delegation refers to the downward transfer of authority from a superior to a subordinate employees. It is a pre-requisite to the efficient functioning of an organisation because it enables a manager to use his/ her time on high priority activities. Importance of delegation is that it helps in effective management, employee development, motivation, growth and coordination.

Elements of Delegation

1. **Authority:** Authority refers to the right to take decisions in order to guide the activities of others. Authority determines the superior subordinate relationship. Laws and the rules and regulations of the organisation restrict authority. Authority flows downward.

2. **Responsibility:** Responsibility is the obligation of a subordinate to perform properly the assigned duty. If the subordinate has the responsibility for a job, he/ she must be given necessary authority to carry out that task.

3. **Accountability:** Accountability implies being accountable for the final outcome. When a superior assigns a work to a subordinate, he/she is answerable to the superior for its outcome

Importance of Delegation

1. **Reduction of Executives' work load:** It reduces the work load of officers. They can thus utilize their time in more important and creative works instead of works of daily routine.

2. **Employee development:** Employees get more opportunities to utilize their talent which allows them to develop those skills which will enable them to perform complex tasks.

3. **Quick and better decision are possible:** The subordinate are granted sufficient authority so they need not to go to their superiors for taking decisions concerning the routine matters.

4. **High Morale of subordinates:** Because of delegation of authority to the subordinates they get an opportunity to display their efficiency and capacity.

5. **Better coordination:** The elements of delegation–authority, responsibility and accountability help to define the powers, duties and answer ability related to various job positions which results in developing and maintaining effective coordination.

Decentralisation: "Decentralisation refers to systematic efforts to delegate to the lowest level, all authority except the one which can be exercised at central points

Importance of Decentralisation

1. Develops initiative among subordinates: It helps to promote confidence and self reliance in the subordinates as they are given freedom to take their own decisions.

2. Develops managerial talent for future: Training given by the organisation and the experience gained from handling the projects increases the talent of the managers and employees.

3. Quick decision making: Since the managerial decisions are taken at all levels nearest to the point of action helps them to take better and quick decisions.

4. Relieves the top management: By the delegation of work, the daily managerial jobs are assigned to the subordinates, which leaves enough time with the superiors to look into priority areas.

Exercise

1. __________ co-ordinates human efforts, assembles resources and integrates both into a unified whole to be utilised for achieving specified objectives.

   (a) Organising   (b) Planning

   (c) Management   (d) Directing

2. Name the third step in the process of organising

   (a) Departmentalisation (b) Division of work

   (c) Establishing duties   (d) Assignment of work

3. Organising is a process by which the manager

   (a) Establishes order out of chaos

   (b) Removes conflict among people over work or responsibility sharing

   (c) Creates an environment suitable for teamwork

   (d) All of the above

4. Organising helps in removing __________ in transfer of information and instructions.

   (a) Ambiguity   (b) Responsibility

   (c) Specification   (d) Clarity

5. The work is divided into manageable activities so that __________ can be avoided and the burden of work can be shared among the employees.

   (a) Identification   (b) Duplication

   (c) Specialisation   (d) All of the above

6. Once work is divided into small activities, similar and related jobs are grouped together. This grouping is called __________

   (a) Departmentalisation (b) Division of work

   (c) Delegation   (d) Assigning duties

7. Establishing authority and responsibility relationship helps to create a __________ structure and also helps in coordination amongst various departments.

   (a) Superior   (b) Hierarchal

   (c) Order   (d) Clarity

8. __________ ensures that the subordinate performs tasks on behalf of the manager thereby reducing his workload and providing him with more time to concentrate on important matters.

   (a) Decentralization   (b) Delegation of authority

   (c) Authority   (d) Accountability

9. The process of organising is __________ which allows a business enterprise to accommodate changes in the business environment.

   (a) Tangible   (b) Flexible

   (c) Stable   (d) None of the above

10. Organising helps in growth and __________ of an enterprise.

    (a) Diversification   (b) Clarification

    (c) Accommodation   (d) Profit

11. The __________ can be defined as the framework within which managerial and operating tasks are performed.

    (a) Span of management

    (b) Directing

    (c) Coordination

    (d) organisation structure

12. Match the column:

    I. Functional structure   A. The organisation structure comprises of separate business units

    II. Formal structure   B. Has no written rules

    III. Divisional structure   C. All departments report to a coordinating head

    IV. Informal structure   D. Specifies clearly the boundaries of authority and responsibility

    Choose the correct option:

    (a) I-C, II-D, III-A, IV-B   (b) I-D, II-B, III-A, IV-A

    (c) I-C, II-A, III-B, IV-D   (d) None of the above

13. __________ refers to the number of subordinates that can be effectively managed by a superior.

    (a) Structure

    (b) Hierarchy

    (c) Span of management

    (d) Managerial function

14. In __________ structure activities are grouped and departments are created on the basis of specific functions to be performed.

    (a) Functional   (b) Divisional

    (c) Managerial   (d) Departmentalisation

15. Jet Airlines Limited has a staff of 200 people which is grouped into different departments. The organisational structure depicts that 100 people work in Production department, 50 in Finance department, 30 in Technology department and 20 in Human Resource department. Identify the type of organisational structure being followed by the company.

    (a) Divisional structure (b) Functional structure

    (c) formal structure   (d) None of the above

16. Functional structure is suitable when the size of the organisation is __________
   (a) Small
   (b) Large
   (c) Operational
   (d) Divisional

17. In a __________ structure, the organisation structure comprises of separate business units or divisions.
   (a) Functional
   (b) Divisional
   (c) Managerial
   (d) Multifunctional

18. Robert has joined as a Content Head in Rio Ltd. An event company. He always ensures that the work has been divided into small and manageable activities and also the activities of similar nature are grouped together. Identify the related step in organising process being mentioned in the above lines.
   (a) Departmentalisation
   (b) Identification and division of work
   (c) Establishing reporting relationships
   (d) Assignment of duties

19. Which of the following is not a demerit of divisional structure
   (a) Promotes flexibility
   (b) Increases costs
   (c) Provides authority
   (d) Conflict of interest

20. Which of the following is not a feature of formal organisation?
   (a) It specifies the relationships among various job positions.
   (b) The standards of behaviour of employees are evolved from group norms.
   (c) It is deliberately designed by the top management.
   (d) It places less emphasis on interpersonal relationships among the employees.

21. Which of the following is/are the merit of formal organisation
   (a) Easier to fix responsibility
   (b) Maintains unity of command
   (c) Provides stability to the organisation
   (d) All of the above

22. Which of the following is not a merit of informal organisation?
   (a) It leads to faster spread of information and speedy feedback.
   (b) It helps to fulfill the social needs of the members.
   (c) It does not fulfill inadequacies in the formal organisation.
   (d) All of the above

Topic Test – I

1. **Assertion (A):** Organising helps in growth of the organisation

   Reasoning (R): It allows business enterprise to add job positions and diversify

   Codes :
   (a) Both Assertion (A) and Reason (R) are true and Reason (R) is the correct explanation of Assertion (A).
   (b) Both Assertion (A) and Reason (R) are true and Reason (R) is not the correct explanation of Assertion (A).
   (c) Assertion (A) is true but Reason (R) is False
   (d) Assertion (A) is False but Reason (R) is true.

2. Organisation structure establishes relationships between
   (a) environment and organisation.
   (b) people, work and resources.
   (c) organisation and society.
   (d) suppliers and customers

3. Organising is a process by which the manager
   (a) Establishes order out of chaos
   (b) Removes conflict among people over work or responsibility sharing
   (c) Creates an environment suitable for teamwork
   (d) All of the above

4. Manhattan Ltd. is a company dealing in Silver products. The work is mainly divided into functions including production, purchase, marketing, accounts etc. Identify the type of organisational structure followed by the organisation.
   (a) managerial structure
   (b) Functional structure
   (c) Divisional structure
   (d) None of the above

5. __________ organisational structure is most suitable when the size of the organisation has diversified activities and operations and require a high degree of specialisation
   (a) Divisional
   (b) Functional
   (c) Network
   (d) None of the above

6. Which of the following is a disadvantage of functional structure
   (a) Gives more importance to the objectives of functional head
   (b) Promotes control
   (c) Reduces duplication
   (d) Increases operational efficiency

7. Identify the correct sequence in the process of organising

   (a) Identification of work, establishing relationship, assignment of duties, departmentalisation

   (b) Departmentalisation, Identification of duties, establishing relationship, assignment of work

   (c) Identification of work, assignment of duties, establishing relationship, departmentalisation

   (d) Identification of work, departmentalisation, assignment of duties, establishing relationship

8. _______ process of controlling ensures that work must be assigned to those who are best fitted to perform it well

   (a) Assignment of duties

   (b) Establishing reporting relationship

   (c) Identification of work

   (d) None of the above

9. State which of the following statement is true

   Statement I: Accountability can be delegated Statement

   Statement II: Responsibility can be delegated completely

   Choose the correct option:

   (a) Statement I is correct and II is wrong

   (b) Statement II is correct and I is wrong

   (c) Both the statements are correct

   (d) Both the statements are incorrect

10. In functional structure, the managerial development is_______

    (a) Difficult   (b) Easy

    (c) Productive   (d) Specialised

11. In a _______ organisation the boundaries of authority & responsibility is clearly defined and there is a systematic coordination among the various activities to achieve organizational objectives.

    (a) Formal

    (b) Informal

    (c) Productive

    (d) Multi product

12. Which of the following is not the advantage of formal organisation.

    (a) Easier to fix responsibility

    (b) Unity of command is maintained

    (c) Avoid duplication of work

    (d) Provide quick solutions

Topic Test – II

1. **Assertion (A):** Identifying and dividing the work is the primary step in the process of organising

   Reasoning (R): Organising avoids duplication of work

   Codes :

   (a) Both Assertion (A) and Reason (R) are true and Reason (R) is the correct explanation of Assertion (A).

   (b) Both Assertion (A) and Reason (R) are true and Reason (R) is not the correct explanation of Assertion (A).

   (c) Assertion (A) is true but Reason (R) is False

   (d) Assertion (A) is False but Reason (R) is true.

2. Interaction among people at work gives rise to a 'network of social relationships among employees' called the _______ organisation.

   (a) Informal   (b) Formal

   (c) Complex   (d) Productive

3. Communication takes place through _______ in formal organisation

   (a) Directly   (b) Planned route

   (c) Scalar chain   (d) In any direction

4. As "The decision making authority is pushed down the chain of command" at G&H enterprises, it provides the benefit of quick decision making to the organisation because:

   (a) There is no requirement for approval from many levels

   (b) Organisation is able to generate more returns

   (c) There are innovative performance systems

   (d) It's a means of management education

5. _______ refers to the downward transfer of authority from a superior to a subordinate employees.

   (a) Authority   (b) Responsibility

   (c) Delegation   (d) Communication

6. _______ implies being accountable for the final outcome.

   (a) Delegation   (b) Accountability

   (c) Superiority   (d) All of the above

7. _______ is the obligation of a subordinate to perform properly the assigned duty.

   (a) Delegation   (b) Responsibility

   (c) Authority   (d) Power

8. Flow of authority is _______.

   (a) Downward   (b) Upward

   (c) Vertical   (d) Free

9. Which of the following is /are the importance of delegation.
   (a) Quick decision making
   (b) Better coordination
   (c) Employee development
   (d) All of the above

10. ________ refers to systematic efforts to delegate to the lowest level, all authority except the one which can be exercised at central points".
    (a) Authority
    (b) Responsibility
    (c) Decentralisation
    (d) Delegation

11. Delegation is a ________ act.
    (a) Compulsory
    (b) Optional policy
    (c) Narrow
    (d) Less control

12. Which of the following is not the importance of decentralisation
    (a) Better control
    (b) Facilitates growth
    (c) It has a narrow scope
    (d) Quick decision making

13. **Assertion (A):** Superior-subordinate relationship leads to responsibility

    Reasoning (R): The subordinate is obligated to perform the job assigned by the superior

    Codes:
    (a) Both Assertion (A) and Reason (R) are true and Reason (R) is the correct explanation of Assertion (A).
    (b) Both Assertion (A) and Reason (R) are true and Reason (R) is not the correct explanation of Assertion (A).
    (c) Assertion (A) is true but Reason (R) is False
    (d) Assertion (A) is False but Reason (R) is true.

Answers

1. (a)	2. (d)	3. (d)	4. (a)	5. (b)	6. (a)	7. (b)	8. (b)	9. (b)	10. (a)
11. (d)	12. (a)	13. (b)	14. (a)	15. (b)	16. (b)	17. (b)	18. a	19. (a)	20. (b)
21. (d)	22. (c)								

Topic – I

1. (a)	2. (b)	3. (d)	4. (b)	5. (b)	6. (a)	7. (d)	8. a	9. (d)	10. (a)
11. (a)	12. (d)								

Topic – II

1. (a)	2. (a)	3. (c)	4. (a)	5. (c)	6. (b)	7. (b)	8. (a)	9. (d	10. (c)
11. (a)	12. (c)	13. (a)							

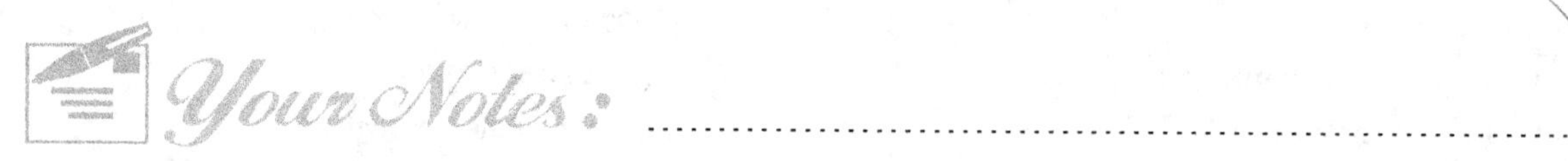
Your Notes :

CHAPTER 6

Staffing

"Staffing is the process of determining the man power requirements that could meet the company's objectives".

Importance of Staffing

1. **Investment costs:** procurement of human resources involves investment in terms of selection, training and development costs.

2. **Holistic Approach:** The usefulness of the persons in an enterprise depends on the managers.

3. **Long Term Effect:** The investment in human resource is of long term effect. This makes the decision to employ and remove a person from employment a very important consideration.

4. **Potential contribution:** while selecting a person more particularly for the managerial position the enterprise has not only to think of the current tastes but also his potential contribution in future.

5. **Multiplier Effect:** The total effect of the functioning of the individual members of a term of managers may not be equal to the effect of the team as a whole.

Process of Staffing

1. Manpower planning
2. Job Analysis
3. Recruitment
4. Selection
5. Placement & Orientation
6. Training
7. Performance Appraisal
8. Promotion & career planning
9. Compensation
10. Separation

Recruitment: is the process of attracting qualified persons to apply for the jobs that are open. It also means finding and attracting capable applicants for employment.

Sources of Recruitment

1. Internal Sources
   - Transfer
     - A. Promotion
     - B. Lay Off
2. External Sources
   - Waiting list
     - A. Recommendations of the present employees
     - B. Notices exhibited in the office, workshop, etc.
     - C. Factory Gate
     - D. Personal consultants
     - E. Media Advertising

Selection: is the process of discovering the most suitable and promising candidates to fill up the position vacant. The intent of the selection process is to gather from applicant's information that will predict their job success.

Steps in selection process

1. Scrutiny of applications received
2. Preliminary application form
3. Specialized application form
4. Testing
5. Interview
6. Checking reference
7. Medical examination
8. Final selection

Training & Development: Training is a learning experience in that it seeks a relatively permanent change in an individual that will improve his ability to perform on the job.

Development is concerned with imparting technical human & conceptual skills. It seeks to develop hidden qualities and talent of persons.

Training methods:

1. Apprenticeship programme
2. Vestibule training
3. Job rotation
4. Internship

Compensation: is what employees receive in exchange for their contribution to the organization. Generally employees offer their services for three types of rewards pay benefits and incentives.

Recruitment: may be defined as the process of searching for prospective employees and stimulating them to apply for jobs in an organization. SOURCES OF RECRUITMENT 1. Internal Sources of Recruitment: Internal sources refer to inviting candidates from within the organization.

External Sources of Recruitment: When the candidates from external sources are invited to fill in the vacant job position then it is known as external recruitment. The common methods of external sources of recruitments are:

1. **Direct Recruitment:** Under the direct recruitment, a notice is put up on the notice board of the enterprise specifying the details of the jobs available.

Types

- **Transfers:** It involves the shifting of an employee from one job to another, from one department to another or from one shift to another shift.

- **Promotions:** It means placing an employee to a higher position carrying higher responsibilities, prestige, facilities and pay.

Advantages

- Employees are motivated to improve their performance.

- Internal recruitment also simplifies the process of selection & placement.

- No wastage of time on the employee training and development.

- Filling of jobs internally is cheaper.

Limitation

- The scope of induction of fresh talent is reduced.

- The employee may become lethargic.

- The spirit of competition among the employees may be hampered.

- Frequent transfers of employees may often reduce the productivity of the organization.

2. **Casual callers:** Many reputed business organizations keep a data base of unsolicited applicants in their office. This list can be screened and best candidate is selected.

3. **Advertisement:** Advertisement media is used when a wider range of candidates to choice are required. Example– Newspapers, Internet, Radio, Television etc.

4. **Employment Exchange:** Employment exchange run by government is regarded as a good source of recruitment for unskilled and skilled operative jobs.

5. **Placement Agencies and Management consultants:** Placement agencies provide a nationwide service in matching personnel demand and supply.

6. **Campus Consultants:** Campus recruitment means recruitment of candidates directly from management and technical institutions and universities.

7. **Labour Contractors:** Labour contractors maintain close contacts with labourers and they can provide the required number of unskilled workers at short notice.

8. **Advertising on Television:** The practice of telecasting of vacant posts over Television is gaining importance these days.

9. **Web Publishing:** There are certain websites specifically designed and dedicated for the purpose of providing information about both job seekers and job opening.

10. **Recommendations of Employees**: Applicants introduced by present employees, or their friends and relatives may prove to be a good source of recruitment.

Merits of External Sources:

The advantages of using external sources of recruitment are as follows:

(i) **Qualified Personnel:** By using external sources of recruitment, the management can attract qualified and trained people to apply for vacant jobs in the organisation.

(ii) **Wider Choice:** When vacancies are advertised widely, a large number of applicants from outside the organisation apply. The management has a wider choice while selecting the people for employment.

(iii) **Fresh Talent:** The present employees may be insufficient or they may not fulfill the specifications of the jobs to be filled. External recruitment provide wider choice and brings new blood in the organisation. However, it is expensive and timeconsuming.

Competitive Spirit: If a company taps external sources, the existing staff will have to compete with the outsiders. They will work harder to show better performance

Limitations of External Sources:

1. **Dissatisfaction among existing staff:** External recruitment may lead to dissatisfaction and frustration among existing employees. They may feel that their chances of promotion are reduced

2. **Lengthy process:** Recruitment from external sources takes a long time. The business has to notify the vacancies and wait for applications to initiate the selection process.

3. **Costly process:** It is very costly to recruit staff from external sources. A lot of money has to be spent on advertisement and processing of applications.

Selection: It can be defined as discovering most promising and most suitable candidate to fill up the vacant job position in the organisation.

Process of Selection:

(i) Preliminary screening

(ii) Selection test

    (a) Intelligence test

    (b) Aptitude test

    (c) Personality test

    (d) Trade test

    (e) Interest test

(iii) Employment interview

(iv) Reference and background cheeks

(v) Selection decision

(vi) Medical examination

(vii) Job offer

(viii) Contract of employment

Training and Development:

(i) **Training:** means equipping the employees with the required skill to perform the job.

(ii) **Development:** It refers to overall growth of the employee. It focuses on personal growth and successful employees development.

Benefits of Training for Organisations:

(i) Reduced learning time

(ii) Better performance

(iii) Attitude formation

(iv) Aids in or help in solving operational problems

(v) Managing manpower need

(vi) Helps to adopt changes

Benefits of Training for Employees:

(i) Better career options

(ii) Earning more

(iii) Boost up the morale

(iv) Less chance of accidents

Training Methods:

(i) On the Job Methods

    (a) Apprenticeship programmes

    (b) Coaching

    (c) Internship training

    (d) Job rotation

(ii) Off the Job Methods

    (a) Classroom lectures

    (b) Films

    (c) Case study

    (d) Computer modelling

    (e) Vestibule training

    (f) Programmed instruction

Exercise

1. _________ begins with workforce planning and includes different other function like recruitment, selection, training, development, promotion, compensation and performance appraisal of work force.
   (a) Planning
   (b) Organising
   (c) Staffing
   (d) Coordination

2. Which of the following statement involves importance of staffing
   (a) Improves job satisfaction
   (b) Helps in discovering competent personnel
   (c) Makes higher performance
   (d) All of the above

3. Staffing is a function which _________ need to perform.
   (a) All the managers
   (b) Top level
   (c) Middle level
   (d) Human resource management

4. In staffing function, which combination of activities in sequential order is correct?
   (a) Recruitment, selection, training, placement
   (b) Selection, training, recruitment, placement
   (c) Recruitment, selection, placement, training
   (d) Recruitment, training, selection, placement

5. **Assertion (A):** Staffing is the most elementary drive of organisational performance

   Reasoning (R): No organisation can be successful until it can keep filled the various positions provided for in the organisation with the suitable amount of people

   Codes:
   (a) Both Assertion (A) and Reason (R) are true and Reason (R) is the correct explanation of Assertion (A).
   (b) Both Assertion (A) and Reason (R) are true and Reason (R) is not the correct explanation of Assertion (A)
   (c) Assertion (A) is true but Reason (R) is False
   (d) Assertion (A) is False but Reason (R) is True.

6. _________ may be defined as the process of searching for prospective employees and stimulating them to apply for jobs in the organisation.
   (a) Training
   (b) Development
   (c) Recruitment
   (d) Selection

7. _________ is the process of choosing from among the pool of the prospective job candidates developed at the stage of recruitment.
   (a) Selection
   (b) Training
   (c) Socialisation
   (d) Orientation

8. _________ means evaluating an employee's current and/or past performance as against certain predetermined standards
   (a) Orientation
   (b) Placement
   (c) Performance appraisal
   (d) Providing feedback

9. _________ are an integral part of people's career.
   (a) Staffing
   (b) Organising
   (c) Efficiency
   (d) Promotions

10. _________ may be in the form of direct financial payments like wages, salaries, incentives, commissions and bonuses and indirect payments like employer paid insurance and vacations.
    (a) Appraisal
    (b) Compensation
    (c) Feedback
    (d) None of the above

11. A _________ means salary and wages are paid either daily, weekly or monthly or annually.
    (a) time based plan
    (b) performance based
    (c) number of units
    (d) performance

12. _________ involves shifting of an employee from one job to another, one department to another or from one shift to another, without a substantive change in the responsibilities and status of the employee.
    (a) Transfers
    (b) Selection
    (c) Position
    (d) Validity

13. Transfer is practically a _________ movement of employees.
    (a) New
    (b) Vertical
    (c) Horizontal
    (d) Lower

14. Which of the following is not the merit of internal sources:
    (a) Motivation
    (b) Simplifies the selection process
    (c) Benefit the shifting work force
    (d) The spirit of competition may be hampered

15. Which type of learning is management development concerned with?

(a) Specific job skill development

(b) Multi-skill development

(c) Manual skill development

(d) Inventory development

16. Which of the following is/are the external sources of recruitment

(a) Casual callers

(b) Advertisement

(c) Campus recruitment

(d) All of the above

17. __________ source of recruitment reduces the cost of recruiting workforce in comparison to other sources.

(a) Direct recruitment   (b) Casual callers

(c) Web publishing   (d) Advertisement

18. __________ is the process of identifying and choosing the best person out of a number of prospective candidates for a job.

(a) Recruitment   (b) Training

(c) Selection   (d) None of the above

19. __________ helps the manager eliminate unqualified or unfit job seekers based on the information supplied in the application forms.

(a) Tests

(b) Technology

(c) Preliminary screening

(d) Interview

20. __________ tests measure the existing skills of the individual.

(a) Aptitude   (b) Interest

(c) Personality   (d) Trade

21. __________ tests are used to know the pattern of involvement of a person.

(a) Interest

(b) Interview

(c) Screening

(d) Aptitude

22. Name the step after selection decision in staffing

(a) Job offer

(b) Background check

(c) Contract

(d) Medical examination

23. Match the column:

I.	Intelligence tests	A. provide clues to a person's emotions
II.	Aptitude test	B. measure the existing skills of the individual
III.	Personality test	C. an indicator of a person's ability to make decisions and judgments.
IV.	Trade tests	D. indicates the person's capacity to develop

Choose the correct option:

(a) I-C, II-D, III-A, IV-B

(b) II-C, I-D, IV-A, III-B

(c) I-A, II-B, III-C, IV-D

(d) None of the above

24. Ashish applied for the post of an psychology lecturer in reputed college in Mumbai. After successfully clearing the tests and the interview, he was offered an employment contract containing the terms and conditions, and the date of joining. Identify the steps in the staffing process being described in the above lines.

(a) Background checking

(b) Medical examination

(c) Contract

(d) Job offer

25. __________ is any process by which the aptitudes, skills and abilities of employees to perform specific jobs are increased.

(a) Training   (b) Development

(c) Aptitude   (d) Recruitment

Topic Test – I

1. __________ simulates the work environment by programming a computer to imitate some of the realities of the job and allows learning to take place without the risk.

(a) Computer modelling

(b) Programmed instruction

(c) Tests

(d) Vestibule training

2. __________ method incorporates a prearranged and proposed acquisition of some specific skills or general knowledge.

(a) High cost

(b) Programmed instruction

(c) Training

(d) Case study

3. __________ can provide information and explicitly demonstrate skills that are not easily represented by the other techniques.

   (a) Classroom lectures   (b) Advertisement

   (c) Films   (d) Internship

4. __________ is a joint programme of training in which educational institutions and business firms cooperate.

   (a) Internship training   (b) Job rotation

   (c) Case study   (d) None of the above

5. __________ type of training involves shifting the trainee from one department to another or from one job to another.

   (a) Case study

   (b) Tests

   (c) Preliminary screening

   (d) Job rotation

6. __________ programmes put the trainee under the guidance of a master worker. These are designed to acquire a higher level of skill.

   (a) Apprenticeship   (b) Off the job

   (c) Training   (d) Uniform

7. __________ refers to the learning opportunities designed to help employees grow.

   (a) Development   (b) Performance

   (c) Training   (d) Recruitment

8. Training is a __________ oriented process.

   (a) Career   (b) Job

   (c) Overall   (d) Knowledge

9. __________ is a formal, in-depth conversation conducted to evaluate the applicant's suitability for the job.

   (a) Employment review

   (b) Selection decision

   (c) Job offer

   (d) Medical examination

10. Kashish joined a Beverage processing unit as a factory worker. Since he was expected to work on tough machineries, he was asked to undergo a special training. Identify the training method mentioned above.

   (a) Vestibule training

   (b) Apprenticeship training

   (c) Induction training

   (d) Internship training

11. __________ results in higher responsibilities and hike in salary

   (a) Job rotation   (b) Transfers

   (c) Promotion   (d) All of the above

12. __________ improves the aptitude of an employee.

   (a) Personal training   (b) Development

   (c) Employment   (d) Recruitment

13. Workforce analysis is a part of ______________-

   (a) Estimating man power requirement

   (b) Recruitment

   (c) Training

   (d) Selection

14. ______________ firms help the organisations to recruit technical, professional and managerial personnel.

   (a) Management consultancy

   (b) Government agency

   (c) Campus

   (d) Institutes

Topic Test – II

1. __________ source of recruitment selects fresh talent.

   (a) Preliminary screening

   (b) Campus recruitment

   (c) Advertisement

   (d) None of the above

2. Staffing is seen as a __________ function of management.

   (a) Component   (b) Motivated

   (c) Structural   (d) Generic

3. __________ step involves locating the potential candidate or determining the sources of potential candidates.

   (a) Selection   (b) Training

   (c) Recruitment   (d) Planning

4. __________ source can be used as a good source of filling the vacancies with employees from over-staffed departments.

   (a) Promotions   (b) Placement

   (c) Exchange   (d) Transfers

5. __________ is an internal source of recruitment.

   (a) Promotions   (b) Placement

   (c) Contracts   (d) Advertisement

6. __________ refers to all forms of pay or rewards going to employees.

   (a) Compensation   (b) Training

   (c) Incentives   (d) Policy

7. Which of the following is not a disadvantage of using external sources of recruitment?

   (a) Dissatisfaction among existing staff

   (b) Lengthy process

   (c) The scope for induction of fresh talent is reduced

   (d) Costly process

8. __________ analysis helps in assessing number and types of human resources necessary for the performance of various jobs and accomplishment of organisational objectives.

   (a) Breakeven analysis

   (b) Workload analysis

   (c) Workforce analysis

   (d) All of the above

9. __________ is not the merit of internal sources of recruitment.

   (a) Motivation

   (b) Simplifies the selection process

   (c) Benefits shifting workforce

   (d) Hampers the spirit of competition

10. __________ source of recruitment may bring in a flood of response, and many times, from quite unsuitable candidates.

    (a) Employment exchange

    (b) Advertisement

    (c) Placement agencies

    (d) Screening

11. __________ contractors maintain close contacts with labourers and they can provide the required number of unskilled workers at short notice.

    (a) Labour   (b) Web

    (c) Human resource   (d) None of the above

12. __________ is/are the merits of external recruitment

    (a) Qualified personnel

    (b) Wider choice

    (c) Fresh talent

    (d) All of the above

13. __________ tests is an indicator of a person's learning ability or the ability to make decisions and judgments.

    (a) Aptitude

    (b) Preliminary

    (c) Intelligence

    (d) Personality

Answers

1. (c)	2. (d)	3. (a)	4. (c)	5. (a)	6. (c)	7. (a)	8. (c)	9. (d)	10. (b)
11. (a)	12. (a)	13. (c)	14. (a)	15. (b)	16. (a)	17. (b)	18. (c)	19. (c)	20. (d)
21. (a)	22. (d)	23. (a)	24. (d)	25. (a)					

Topic – I

1. (a)	2. (b)	3. (c)	4. (a)	5. (d)	6. (a)	7. (a)	8. (b)	9. (a)	10. (a)
11. (c)	12. (b)	13. (a)	14. (a)						

Topic – II

1. (b)	2. (d)	3. (c)	4. (d)	5. (a)	6. (a)	7. (c)	8. (b)	9. (d)	10. (b)
11. (a)	12. (d)	13. (c)							

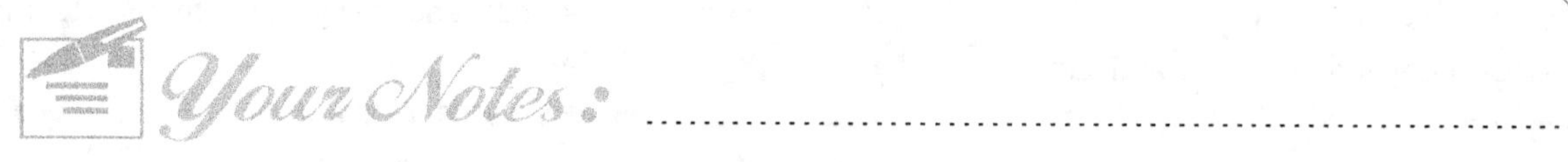
Your Notes :

CHAPTER 7

Directing

"Directing means giving instructions and guiding people in doing work. It refers to the process of instructing, guiding, counselling motivating and leading people in the organization to achieve its objectives".

Characteristics of Directing:

1. Directing initiates action- A manager has to perform this function along with planning, organising, staffing and controlling while discharging his duties in the organisation.

2. Directing takes place at every level of management- Every manager, from top executive to supervisor performs the function of directing.

3. It is a continuous process- It takes place throughout the life of the organisation irrespective of people occupying managerial positions

4. It flows from top to bottom- It means that every manager can direct his immediate subordinate and take instructions from his immediate boss

Importance of Directing:

1. It initiates action towards attainment of desired objectives.

2. It integrates employees efforts

3. It guides employees to realize their potential and capabilities

4. It facilitates introduction of needed changes.

5. Effective directing helps to bring stability and balance.

Principles of Directing

1. **Maximum individual contribution:** This principle emphasises that directing techniques must help every individual in the organisation to contribute to his maximum potential for achievement of organisational objectives.

2. **Harmony of objectives:** It is an important function of management to motivate people and direct their efforts towards the achievement of enterprise objectives and their personal goals. The interest of the group must always prevail over individual interest. The principle implies harmony of personal interest and common interest.

3. **Unity of command:** This principle states that one person should receive orders from only one superior, in other words, one person should be accountable to only one boss.

4. **Appropriateness of direction technique:** Appropriate motivational and leadership technique should be used by a manger while directing the people based on subordinate needs, capabilities, attitudes and other situational variables.

5. **Managerial communication:** Directing should convey clear instructions to subordinates and proper feedback ensure that they understood the instructions clearly.

6. **Use of informal organization:** A manager should realise that informal groups or organisations exist within every formal organisation.

7. **Leadership:** While directing the subordinates, managers should exercise good leadership as it can influence the subordinates positively without causing dissatisfaction among them.

8. **Follow up:** A manager not only issue orders and instructions, but also follow-up the performance employees so as to ensure that work is being performed as desired. He should intelligently oversee his subordinates at work and correct them whenever they go wrong.

Elements of Directing:

1. Supervision

2. Motivation

3. Leadership

4. Communication

Supervision: is the process of guiding the efforts of employees and other resources to accomplish the desired objectives.

Importance of supervision

1. Supervisor plays a key role maintain a group unity among workers.

2. Supervisor acts as link between workers and management.

3. Influences the workers by his leadership quality.

4. Analyses the work performed and gives feedback.

Motivation: means the process of making subordinates to act in a desired manner to achieve certain organizational goals.

i. Motive: A motive is an inner state that energises, activates or moves and directs behaviour towards goals.

ii. Motivation: Motivation is the process of stimulating people to action to accomplish desired goals.

iii. Motivator: is the technique used to motivate people in an organisation

Features of motivation:

1. Produces goal directed behaviour

2. Can be positive or negative.

3. Is an internal feeling

4. Is a complex process

Importance of Motivation:

1. Helps to improve performance of employees as well as organisation.

2. Helps to reduce employee turnover

3. Helps to change indifferent attitudes of employees

4. Helps to reduce absenteeism in the organisation

5. Facilitate change

Maslow's Need Heirarchy Theory of Motivation:

1. **Basic Physiological Needs:** These are the most basic need such as food, shelter, sleep etc. In the organisational context, basic salary helps to satisfy these needs.

2. **Safety/ Security Need:** Provide security from physical and emotional harm E.g. Job security, stability Etc.

3. **Affiliation/ Belonging Need:** These needs refer to affection, sense of belongingness, acceptance

4. **Esteem Needs:** These include factors such as self-respect, prestige, autonomy status, recognition and attention.

5. **Self Actualisation Needs:** It is the highest level of need in the hierarchy. It refers to the drive to become what one is capable of becoming.

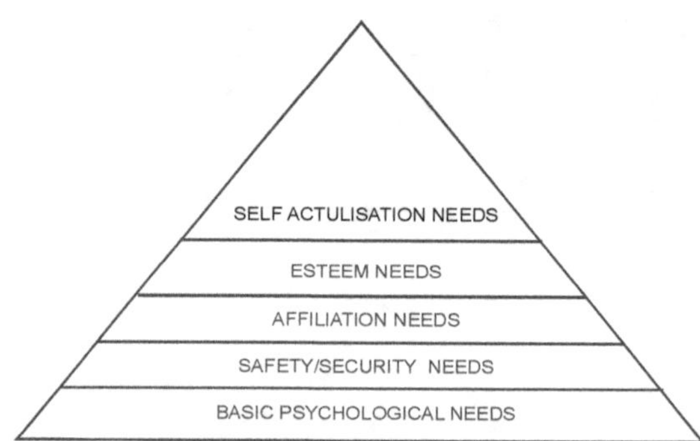

Incentives: means all the measures which are used to motivate people to improve performance. There are two types of incentives

(A) **Financial incentive:** Financial incentives refer to incentives which are in direct monetary form or measurable in monetary term and serve to motivate people for better performance.

Types of Financial Incentive:

i. **Pay and allowance:** For every employee/ worker, salary is the basic monetary incentive.

ii. **Productivity linked wage incentives:** In this the payment of wages is determined on the basis of the goods produced.

iii. **Bonus:** Bonus is an incentive offered over and above the wages/ salary to the employees.

iv. **Profit Sharing:** Profit sharing is meant to provide a share to employees in the profits of the organisation in order to motivate them.

v. **Co-partnership/ Stock option:** Under these incentive schemes, employees of the company are given an option to buy the company shares at a set price which is lower than market price.

vi. **Retirement Benefits:** Retirement benefits are the benefits received either at the time of retirement or afterwards, such as provident fund, pension, and gratuity.

(B) **Non-financial incentives:** refers to reward that doesn't form part of salary/ wage of the employee. It provides psychological satisfaction to an employee.

i. Status

ii. Organisational climate

iii. Career advancement opportunity

iv. Job enrichment

v. Job security

vi. Employee participation

vii. Employee empowerment

Leadership: process of influencing the behaviour of people by making them strives voluntarily towards achievement of organizational goals.

Features of leadership:

i. Leadership indicates ability of an individual to influence others.

ii. Leadership tries to bring change in the behaviour of others.

iii. Leadership indicates interpersonal relations between leaders and followers.

iv. Leadership is exercised to achieve common goals of the organisation.

v. Leadership is a continuous process.

Importance of leadership:

i. Influences the behaviour of people positively.

ii. Handle conflicts effectively

iii. Maintains personal relations and followers in fulfilling their needs.

iv. Play key role in introducing changes in an enterprise.

Qualities of a good leader:

1. Knowledge
2. Integrity
3. Initiative
4. Communication skills
5. Social skills
6. Self confidence

Leadership Style:

I. **Autocratic or Authoritarian Style:** autocratic leader give orders and expect them to obey them. If a manager is following this style, then communication is only one-way with the subordinate only acting according to the command given by the manager.

II. **Democratic or Participative:** a democratic leader gives order after consulting the group and works out the policies with acceptance of the group. It works best in the situations where group member is skilled and competent to share their knowledge.

III. **Laissez-faire or free rein:** the followers are given a high degree of independence to formulate their own objectives and ways to achieve them.

Communication: refers to process of exchange of ideas between on among persons and create understanding.

In an organization both formal and informal communication also exists.

Importance of Communication

1. **Basis of coordination:** facilitates coordination between various departments and sections thus creating a unity of purpose and action.

2. **Basis of decision making:** Communication provides needed information for decision making. In its absence, it may not be possible for the managers to take any meaningful decision.

3. **Increases managerial efficiency:** Communication is essential for quick and effective performance of managerial functions. The management conveys the goals and targets, issues instructions, allocates jobs and responsibilities and looks after the performance of subordinates.

4. **Boosts morale and provides motivation:** An efficient system of communication enables management to motivate, influence and satisfy the subordinates.

Formal Communication: flows through official channels designed in the organisation chart. There is a two-way information flow between the superior and subordinates. The communications may be oral or written but generally recorded and filed in the office.

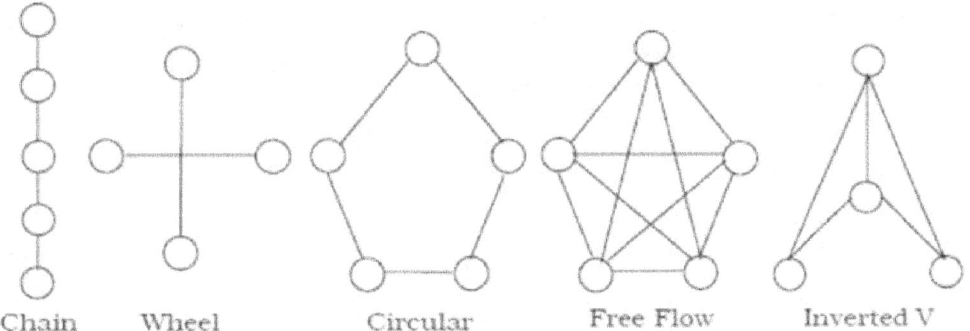

Informal Communication: Communication that takes place without following the formal lines of communication is said to be informal communication. Informal communication is sometimes called the grapevine as it spreads throughout the organisation and might be observed occurring in conversations, electronic mails, text messages and phone calls between socializing employees.

GRAVEVINE COMMUNICATION NETWORK

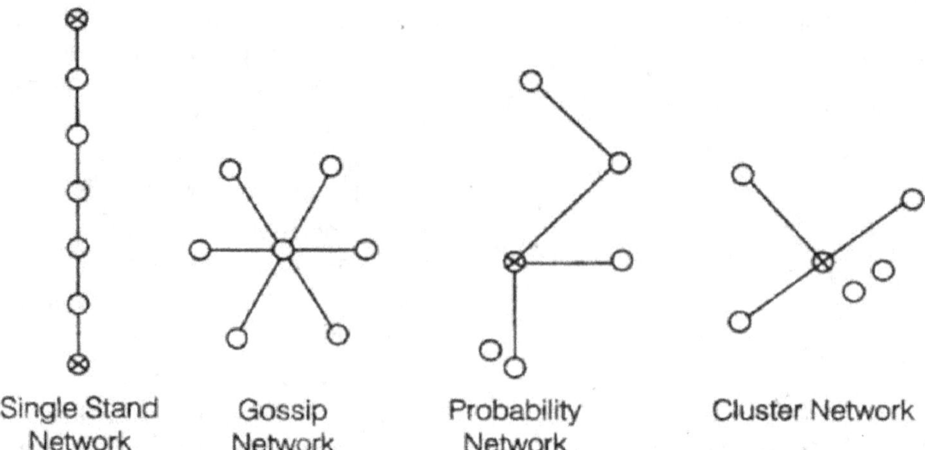

Barriers to communication:

1. **Semantic barrier:** Concerned with communication problems and obstructions in the process of encoding or decoding of message into words.

   i. **Badly expressed message:** some intended meaning may not be conveyed by the usage of inadequate vocabulary, wrong meaning, words, etc.

   ii. **Symbols with different meaning:** words with different meanings confuse the receiver.

   iii. **Faulty transactions:** The meaning of a message in one language if translated will be different in other language.

   iv. **Unclarified assumption:** Different assumptions may have different interpretations, which result in confusion.

   v. **Technical Jargon:** Usage of technical words by specialists will result in misunderstanding among workers.

   vi. **Body language and gesture decoding:** Every movement of body communicates a meaning.

2. **Psychological barrier:** Some of the psychological barriers are:

   1. **Premature evaluation:** judgement before listening leads to misunderstanding.

   2. **Lack of attention:** poor listening due to preoccupied mind of the receiver may disappoint the sender.

   3. **Loss by transmission and poor retention:** When oral communication passes through various channels of communication, it destroys the structure of the message or leads to transmission of inaccurate message.

   4. **Distrust:** If the parties do not believe each other, they cannot understand each other's message in its original sense.

3. **Organisational barrier:** If the organisation policy is not supportive of free flow of communication it disrupts effectiveness of communication.

   1. Organizational policy
   2. Rules & Regulations
   3. Status
   4. Complexity in the organisation structure
   5. Organisational facilities

Exercise

1. Which of the following is not a characteristic of directing
   (a) Initiates action
   (b) Takes place at all levels of management
   (c) Is a continuous process
   (d) Flows from bottom to top

2. __________ refers to the process of instructing, guiding, counselling, motivating and leading people in the organisation to achieve their objectives.
   (a) Planning
   (b) Organising
   (c) Staffing
   (d) Directing

3. Which of the following is an element of directing?
   (a) Supervision
   (b) Communication
   (c) Leadership
   (d) All of the above

4. __________ isdefined as the process of guiding the efforts of employees and other resources to accomplish the desired objectives.
   (a) Communication
   (b) Supervision
   (c) Leadership
   (d) Motivation

5. State which of the following statement is true
   Statement I: Directing flows from top to bottom:
   Statement II: Directing is a key managerial function.
   Choose the correct option:
   (a) Statement I is correct and II is wrong
   (b) Statement II is correct and I is wrong
   (c) Both the statements are correct
   (d) Both the statements are incorrect

6. __________ introduced the need hierarchy theory of motivation
   (a) Maslow
   (b) Fayol
   (c) Taylor
   (d) None of the above

7. Which one of the following is a financial incentive?
   (a) Extra allowance
   (b) Provident Fund
   (c) Bonus
   (d) All of the above

8. Directing is a__________ process.
   (a) Continuous
   (b) Lengthy
   (c) Short
   (d) Single day

9. Self actualisation needs are concerned with__________
   (a) Growth
   (b) Self fulfilment
   (c) Both a and b
   (d) Neither a nor b

10. Atul works as manager in 'VBC ltd.' He has been given the best employee award as he was able to integrate group efforts and was able to get maximum out of his subordinates. Which function is performed by Atul ?
    (a) Directing
    (b) Organising
    (c) Staffing
    (d) None of the above

11. __________ is the process of guiding the efforts of employees and other resources to accomplish the desired objectives.
    (a) Motivation
    (b) Supervision
    (c) Directing
    (d) Coordination

12. In an organisation, Mr. Kapoor is the supervisor and has 15 subordinates under him. He communicates with all the subordinates in a single line.__________ type of network is followed by them
    (a) Free flow
    (b) Scalar chain
    (c) Wheel
    (d) Single chain

13. Two way communication technique is used under__________
    (a) Autocratic style
    (b) Democratic
    (c) Free flow
    (d) None of the above

14. Which of the following is a leadership style
    (a) Autocratic
    (b) Democratic
    (c) Free rein
    (d) All of the above

15. Grapevine is a form of
    (a) Communication barrier
    (b) Formal communication
    (c) Informal communication
    (d) None of the above

16. Guess the type of communication shown in the picture:

    (a) Wheel
    (b) Free flow
    (c) Inverted
    (d) Chain

17. In__________type of communication each person can communicate with his adjoining two persons.
    (a) Inverted
    (b) Circular
    (c) Wheel
    (d) Single chain

18. These__________ messages may be an account of inadequate vocabulary, usage of wrong words, omission of needed words, etc

(a) Badly expressed   (b) Omitted

(c) Faulty   (d) None of the above

19. Assertion (A): Informal communication appears from social interaction of people

Reasoning: The information system of communication is called as grapevine

Codes :

(a) Both Assertion (a) and Reason (R) are true and Reason (R) is the correct explanation of Assertion (A).

(b) Both Assertion (a) and Reason (R) are true and Reason (R) is not the correct explanation of Assertion (A).

(c) Assertion (A) is true but Reason (R) is False

(d) Assertion (A) is False but Reason (R) is True.

20. Which of the following is an element of directing

(a) Delegating authority

(b) Designing organisation structure

(c) Communication

(d) Designing control system

Topic Test – I

1. Which of the following is not a characteristic of directing?

(a) Directing initiate action

(b) It is a continuous process

(c) Flows from top to bottom

(d) Ensuring order & discipline

2. Which of the following is the elements of directing?

(a) Supervision   (b) Motivation

(c) Leadership   (d) All of the above

3. __________ is the process of guiding the efforts of employees to accomplish the desired goal.

(a) Supervision   (b) Directing

(c) Controlling   (d) Motivating

4. Which of the following is not a non-financial incentive?

(a) Status   (b) Job enrichment

(c) Bonus   (d) Employee progress

5. Which of the following is not a feature of motivation?

(a) It is an integral feeling

(b) Reduces absenteeism

(c) Complex process

(d) Can be positive or negative

6. Assertion (A): Directing is all pervasive

Reasoning (R): Directing is continuous even if there is any change in the management as organisational activities cannot continue further without direction

Codes :

(a) Both Assertion (A) and Reason (R) are true and Reason (R) is the correct explanation of Assertion (A).

(b) Both Assertion (A) and Reason (R) are true and Reason (R) is not the correct explanation of Assertion (A)

(c) Assertion (A) is true but Reason (R) is False

(d) Assertion (A) is False but Reason (R) is True

7. __________ is the process of influencing the behaviour of people making them strive voluntarily towards achievement of goals

(a) Motivation   (b) Communication

(c) Leadership   (d) Directing

8. Informal communication is also called:

(a) Wheel communication

(b) Grapevine

(c) Verbal

(d) Visual

9. Encoding is related to _____________

(a) Converting message into symbols.

(b) Converting symbols into machine

(c) Transmitting message

(d) Receiving symbols

10. __________ is the process of stimulating people towards goal-oriented behaviour.

(a) Communication   (b) Motivation

(c) Directing   (d) None of these

Topic Test – II

1. Which of the following is not a type of personal barrier

(a) Fear of challenge to authority .

(b) Unwillingness to communicate

(c) Loss by transmission and poor retention

(d) Lack of proper incentive

2. Identify the type of network

(a) Gossip   (b) Single chain

(c) Wheel   (d) Inverted v

3. Which of the leadership style yields the advantage of high level motivation

(a) Free rein   (b) Autocratic

(c) Democratic   (d) None of the above

4. Motivation is said to be__________

(a) Positive

(b) Negative

(c) Both (a) and (b)

(d) Neither (a) nor (b)

5. The process of concerting the message into communication symbols is known as

(a) Receiving   (b) Sending

(c) Media   (d) Encoding

6. Identify the type of communication:

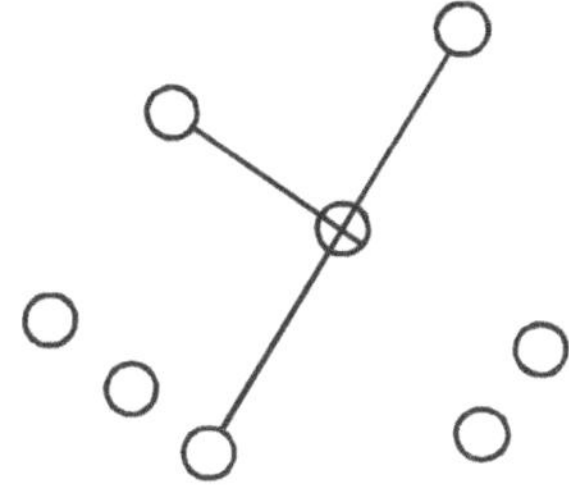

(a) Probability

(b) Cluster

(c) Gossip

(d) Wheel

7. Psychological needs include:

(a) Food   (b) House

(c) Clothes   (d) All of the above

8. Effective motivation in the organisation does not contribute towards

(a) Developing performance levels of employees

(b) Helping to reduce employee turnover

(c) Resistance to changes in the organisation

(d) All of the above

9. State which of the following statement is true

Statement I: Semantics is the branch of linguistics dealing with the meaning of words and sentences.

Statement II: Some times people evaluate the meaning of message before the sender completes his message

Choose the correct option:

(a) Statement I is correct and II is wrong

(b) Statement II is correct and I is wrong

(c) Both the statements are correct

(d) Both the statements are incorrect

10. __________ rules and cumbersome procedures may be a hurdle to communication.

(a) Rigid   (b) flexible

(c) channelled   (d) none of the above

Answers

1. (d)	**2.** (d)	**3.** (d)	**4.** (b)	**5.** (c)	**6.** (a)	**7.** (d)	**8.** (a)	**9.** (c)	**10.** (a)
11. (b)	**12.** (d)	**13.** (b)	**14.** (d)	**15.** (c)	**16.** (a)	**17.** (b)	**18.** (a)	**19.** (b)	**20.** (c)

Topic – I

1. (d)	**2.** (d)	**3.** (a)	**4.** (c)	**5.** (b)	**6.** (b)	**7.** (c)	**8.** (b)	**9.** (a)	**10.** (b)

Topic – II

1. (c)	**2.** (a)	**3.** (a)	**4.** (c)	**5.** (d)	**6.** (b)	**7.** (d)	**8.** (c)	**9.** (c)	**10.** (a)

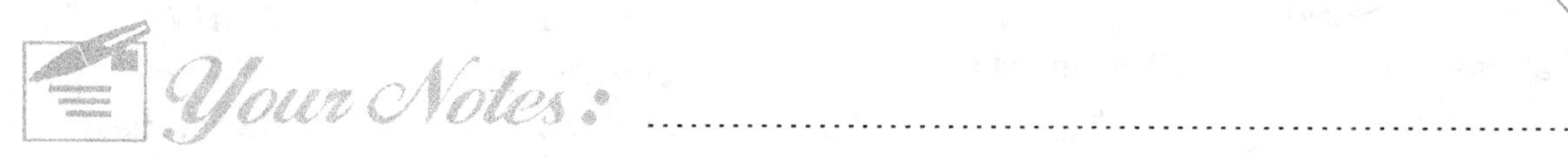
Your Notes :

CHAPTER 8

Controlling

Summary

Controlling means ensuring that activities in an organization are performed as per the plans. It also ensures that organization resources are being used effectively and efficiently for the achievement of pre-determined goals.

Importance of Controlling

1. Accomplishing organizational goals
2. Judging accuracy of standards
3. Making efficient use of resources
4. Improving employee motivation
5. Ensuring order & discipline

Limitations of Controlling:

1. **Difficulty in setting quantitative standards:** Control system loses some of its effectiveness when standards cannot be quantified.
2. **Little control on external factors:** An organisation cannot control external factors such as government policies, technological changes, competition etc.
3. **Resistance from employees:** Mostly employees resist controlling by managers.
4. **Costly affair:** Control is a costly process as it involves a lot of expenditure, time and effort.

Relationship between Planning and Controlling

1. Planning provides base for controlling
2. Planning is theoretical whereas controlling is practical
3. Planning is looking ahead and controlling is looking back.

Process of Controlling

1. **Setting performance standards:** The first step in the controlling process is setting an performance standards which can be compared with actual performance

2. **Measurement of Actual performance:** should be measured in an objective & reliable manner. These include sample checking performance reports, etc.
3. **Comparing Actual performance with standards:** This is done to know the status of deviation for necessary action.
4. **Analyzing deviation:** some deviations in performance can be expected in all activities therefore it is important to determine the acceptable range of deviations.
5. **Taking corrective action:** Remedial actions are taken to prevent deviation in future and improve the performance.

Techniques of Managerial Control

Traditional Techniques	Modern Techniques
1. Personal Observation	1. Return on investment
2. Statistical Reports	2. Ratio Analysis
3. Breakeven Analysis	3. Responsibility Accounting
	4. Management Audit
	5. PERT & CPM

Traditional Techniques:

1. **Personal Observation**: It enables the manager to collect first hand information but it is very time consuming and cannot be used in all kinds of job.
2. **Statistical Reports:** Statistical analysis in the form of averages, percentages, ratios, correlation, etc., present useful information to the managers regarding performance of the organisation.
3. **Breakeven analysis:** is a technique to study the relationship between costs, volume and profits
4. **Budgetary Control:** is a technique of managerial control in which all activities are planned in advance in the form of budgets and actual results are compared with budgetary standards.

II. Modern Techniques

1. **Return on Investment**: Return on Investment (ROI) is a technique which provides the basic yardstick for measuring whether or not invested capital has been used effectively for generating reasonable amount of return.

2. **Ratio Analysis:** Ratio Analysis refers to analysis of financial statements by computation of various ratios.

   1. Liquidity Ratios
   2. Solvency Ratios
   3. Profitability Ratios
   4. Turnover Ratios

Management Audit: Management audit refers to systematic performance appraisal of the management of an organisation.

PERT & CPM: Program Evaluation and Review Technique and critical path method techniques help in execution of projects within given schedule structure of costs of planning , scheduling & implementing time bound projects.

Management Information System

It is defined as assembling of facilities and personnel for collecting, processing, storing, retrieving and transmitting information that is required by one or more managers in the performance of their functions. It provides information of different levels of management and across different departments of organization.

It supports planning, decision making and controlling.

Exercise

1. __________ means ensuring that activities in an organisation are performed as per the plans
   - (a) Planning
   - (b) Coordinating
   - (c) Organising
   - (d) Controlling

2. Controlling is a __________ function
   - (a) Goal – oriented
   - (b) Organisational
   - (c) Quantitative
   - (d) Career oriented

3. Which of the following is not an importance of controlling function?
   - (a) It ensures order and discipline.
   - (b) It restricts co-ordination in action.
   - (c) It helps in judging accuracy of standards.
   - (d) It improves employee motivation.

4. Controlling is said to be a costly affair. Justify the statement as
   - (a) True
   - (b) False
   - (c) Partially true
   - (d) Partially false

5. Controlling function leads the management back to
   - (a) Directing
   - (b) Staffing
   - (c) Planning
   - (d) Coordination

6. State which of the following statement is true

   Statement I: Planning based on facts makes controlling easier and effective

   Statement II: Controlling improves future planning by providing information derived from past experience.

   Choose the correct option:
   - (a) Statement I is correct and II is wrong
   - (b) Statement II is correct and I is wrong
   - (c) Both the statements are correct
   - (d) Both the statements are incorrect

7. Arrange the following steps in the process of controlling in the correct sequence:
   - (a) Setting performance standards
   - (b) Measurement of actual performance
   - (c) Analysing deviations
   - (d) Comparison of actual performance with standards
   - (e) Taking corrective action
   - i. a, b, d, e, c
   - ii. a, b, d, c, e
   - iii. a, b, c, d, e
   - iv. b, a, c, e, d

8. "Standards can be set in both quantitative as well as qualitative terms."
   - (a) True
   - (b) False
   - (c) Partially true
   - (d) None of the above

9. Personal observation, sample checking, performance reports, helps in __________ process of controlling
   - (a) Analysing deviations
   - (b) Taking corrective actions
   - (c) Measurement of actual performance
   - (d) Setting the standards

10. __________ is an important principle of management control based on the belief that an attempt to control everything results in controlling nothing.
    - (a) Management by exception
    - (b) Critical point
    - (c) Deviations
    - (d) Inadequacy

11. Match the following cause of deviation by corrective action to be taken

I.	Defective material	A.	modify the existing process
II.	Obsolete machinery	B.	change the quality specification
III.	Defective process	C.	undertake technological upgradation

    Choose the correct option:
    - (a) I-C, II-A, III-B
    - (b) I-B, III-C, III-A
    - (c) I-C, II-A, III-B
    - (d) I-A, II-B, III-C

12. __________ techniques have not become obsolete and are still being used by companies.
    - (a) Traditional
    - (b) Managerial
    - (c) Modern
    - (d) All of the above

13. __________ is the most traditional method of control.
    - (a) Break even analysis
    - (b) Accounting
    - (c) PERT
    - (d) Personal observation

14. In a marketing firm, the Financial Manager Robert pays more attention towards an increase of 5% in the marketing cost as compared to a 10% increase in the courier expenses. Identify the concept being used by the manager.
    - (a) Critical point control
    - (b) Deviations
    - (c) Corrective action
    - (d) management control

15. __________ provides the required information to the managers by systematically processing a massive data generated in an organisation.
    - (a) Functions
    - (b) Management information system
    - (c) Deviations and standards
    - (d) Network

16. __________ are used extensively in areas like ship-building, construction projects, aircraft manufacture, etc.

(a) PERT & CPM   (b) MIS

(c) Statistics   (d) Network diagram

17. __________ helps to locate present and potential deficiencies in the performance of management functions.

(a) MIS   (b) CPM

(c) Management audit   (d) None of the above

18. "Planning and controlling are inseparable twins of management."

(a) True   (b) False

(c) Partially true   (d) Partially false

19. __________ is not the limitation of controlling

(a) Difficult in setting quantitative standards

(b) Little control on external factors

(c) Resistance from employees

(d) Efficient use of resources

20. __________ serve as benchmarks towards which an organisation strives to work.

(a) Performance   (b) Action

(c) Deviation   (d) Standard

Topic Test – I

1. Assertion (A): Controlling helps to reduce wastage of resources

Reasoning (R): Efficient control system creates an environment of order in an organisation

Codes:

(a) Both Assertion (A) and Reason (R) are true and Reason (R) is the correct explanation of Assertion (A).

(b) Both Assertion (A) and Reason (R) are true and Reason (R) is not the correct explanation of Assertion (A)

(c) Assertion (A) is true but Reason (R) is False

(d) Assertion (A) is False but Reason (R) is True.

2. Which of the following statements does not highlight the relationship between planning and controlling?

(a) Planning and controlling are separable twins of management.

(b) Planning without controlling is meaningless, controlling without planning is blind.

(c) Planning is prescriptive, controlling is evaluative.

(d) Planning and controlling are interrelated and interdependent.

3. The controlling function is performed by:

(a) Top level   (b) Middle level

(c) Supervisors   (d) All of the above

4. __________ is the difference between standard performance and actual performance'.

(a) KRA's   (b) Results

(c) Process   (d) Deviations

5. "These techniques provide a refreshingly new thinking on the ways in which various aspects of an organisation can be controlled".

(a) Traditional   (b) Performance

(c) Modern   (d) Standard

6. Mr. Kapoor, Manager of pharmaceutical company attempt to determine the difference between actual number of product sold and the desired amount. He was very well aware of the standards laid. Identify the process of controlling.

(a) Analysing deviations

(b) Measurement of actual performance

(c) Comparing the standards and actual performance

(d) None of the above

7. Mr. Arun is familiar with the fact that good control system helps to minimise dishonest behaviour on the part of the employee by keeping an eye on their activities. Which importance of controlling is expressed above:

(a) Accomplishing organisational goals

(b) Improving employee motivation

(c) Ensuring order and discipline

(d) Coordination on action

8. "Justify the statement planning and controlling are both backward-looking as well as a forward-looking function".

(a) True   (b) False

(c) Partially true   (d) Partially false

9. __________ in the form of averages, percentages, ratios, correlation, etc., present useful information to the managers regarding performance of the organisation in various areas.

(a) Deviations   (b) Statistical analysis

(c) Comparison   (d) None of the above

10. __________ is a useful technique for the managers as it helps in estimating profits at different levels of activities.

(a) Breakeven analysis (b) Statistical reports

(c) Cost curve   (d) Demand curve

Topic Test – II

1. Measurement of performance and their comparison with standards is a tough job in case of human behaviour. Which limitation of controlling is mentioned above
   - (a) Costly affairs
   - (b) Diificult in setting quantitative standards
   - (c) Resistance from employee
   - (d) None of the above

2. Budgetary control requires the preparation of
   - (a) Statistics
   - (b) Cost curve
   - (c) Budgets
   - (d) All of the above

3. **Assertion (A):** Controlling helps in achieving pre determined goals by utilising the resources effectively and efficiency

   Reasoning (R): It is both forward and backward looking function

   Codes :
   - (a) Both Assertion (A) and Reason (R) are true and Reason (R) is the correct explanation of Assertion (A).
   - (b) Both Assertion (A) and Reason (R) are true and Reason (R) is not the correct explanation of Assertion (A)
   - (c) Assertion (A) is true but Reason (R) is False
   - (d) Assertion (A) is False but Reason (R) is True.

4. __________ means ensuring that activities in an organisation are performed as per the plans.
   - (a) Planning
   - (b) Coordination
   - (c) Functional management
   - (d) Controlling

5. __________ is the focus point for a manager while controlling, as controlling at every step is not possible
   - (a) Controlling
   - (b) Coordinating
   - (c) Critical point control
   - (d) Both (a) and (b)

6. __________ refers to analysis of financial statements through computation of ratios.
   - (a) Return on investment
   - (b) Ratio Analysis
   - (c) Performance
   - (d) Amount of return

7. A __________ centre is a segment of an organisation in which managers are held responsible for the cost incurred in the centre but not for the revenues.
   - (a) Cost
   - (b) Profit
   - (c) Revenue
   - (d) Investment

8. Gross Profit, Ratio Net Profit Ratio , Return on Capital Employed are the example of __________ ratio.
   - (a) Liquidity
   - (b) Solvency
   - (c) Turnover
   - (d) Profitability

9. __________ is a segment of an organisation whose manager is responsible for both revenues and costs.
   - (a) Cost centre
   - (b) Profit centre
   - (c) Investment centre
   - (d) Revenue centre

10. __________ techniques deals with time scheduling and resource allocation for these activities and aims at effective execution of projects within given time schedule and structure of costs.
    - (a) PERT AND CPM
    - (b) PERT
    - (c) CPM
    - (d) Network diagram

Answers

1. (d)	2. (a)	3. (b)	4. (a)	5. (c)	6. (c)	7. (b)	8. (a)	9. (c)	10. (a)
11. (b)	12. (a)	13. (d)	14. (a)	15. (b)	16. (a)	17. (c)	18. (a)	19. (d)	20. (d)

Topic – I

1. (d)	2. (a)	3. (d)	4. (d)	5. (c)	6. (c)	7. (c)	8. (a)	9. (b)	10. (a)

Topic – II

1. (b)	2. (c)	3. (b)	4. (d)	5. (c)	6. (b)	7. (a)	8. (d)	9. (b)	10. (a)

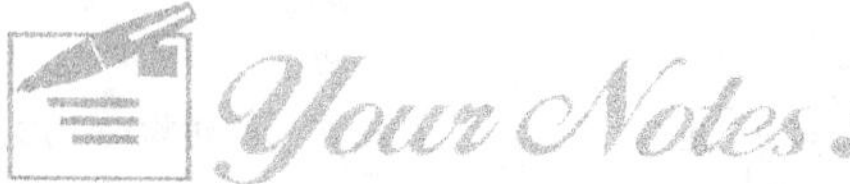 Your Notes: ....

CHAPTER 9

Financial Management

Financial management is concerned with managerial activities relating to planning, procurement and administration of funds and their optimum utilization.

Objectives of financial management

1. Procurement of necessary funds at economic costs-
2. Appreciation in the value of funds
3. Coordination between different departments of the enterprise
4. Financial control to ensure the safety of funds

Financial Decision

It can be categorised as Investment decision , financing and dividend decision.

I. Investment Decision: Investment decision means judicious investment of firm's resources, from the available alternative proposals and choosing the cheapest one, which earns highest possible return for the investors. Investment decisions are decisions about how the firm's funds are invested in different assets that is, in different investment proposals.

    A. Long term decision

    B. Short term decision

Factors Affecting Capital Budgeting Decisions

1. **Cash flows of the project:** a series of cash receipts and payments over the life of an investment proposal is considered and analyzed for selecting the best proposal.

2. **The Rate of Return:** The calculation of expected returns from each proposal and risk involved is taken into account to select the best proposal.

3. **The Investment Criteria Involved:** Various investment proposals are evaluated, based on capital budgeting techniques. These involve calculation regarding investment amount, cash flows, rate of return etc.

II. Financing Decision: Financing decision aids in identifying various sources of the funds and select the best one by evaluating the different characteristics of the funds available and its impact on the firm's capital structure and returns. This decision is about the quantum of finance to be raised from various long-term sources and short-term sources and selecting the cheapest one.

Factors affecting financial decision

1. Cost
2. Risk
3. Cash Flow Positions
4. Floatation Cost

III. Dividend Decision: Dividend is that portion of divisible profits that is distributed to the shareholders. It results in current income for the shareholders. The dividend decisions are taken keeping in view the overall objective of maximizing shareholder's wealth.

Factors Affecting Dividend Decision:

a. Amount of earnings
b. Stability of dividends
c. Growth opportunities
d. Cash flow positions
e. Shareholder preferences
f. Taxation policy
g. Stock market reaction
h. Access to capital market
i. Legal constraints
j. Contractual constraints

Financial planning

Financial planning refers to planning regarding financial needs of the enterprise various sources of raising funds and their optimum utilization.

Objectives of financial planning

a. **To ensure availability of funds whenever required:** Includes proper estimation of the funds required for different purposes (long term assets/ working cap requirement). There is a need to estimate the time at which these funds are to be made available. Financial planning also tries to specify possible sources of these funds.

b. To see that the firm does not raise resources unnecessarily: Excess funding is as bad as inadequate funding. Surplus funds reduces return and increases cost to a company.

Importance of Financial Planning

1. It facilitates collection of optimum funds.
2. It helps in fixing the most appropriate capital structure.
3. Helps in investing finance in right project.
4. Helps in operational activities & reduces financial uncertainties.
5. Link between investment and financial decision

Capital structure: Factors Determining The Capital Structure

1. Cash flow ability
2. Control
3. Flexibility
4. Cost of Debt
5. Market Conditions
6. Flotation Costs
7. Interest Coverage Ratio

Factors Affecting the Choice of Capital Structure

a. Cash flow position
b. Interest coverage ratio
c. Debt service coverage ratio
d. Return on investment
e. Cost of debt
f. Tax rate
g. Cost of equity
h. Floatation cost
i. Flexibility
j. Risk consideration
k. Control
l. Stock market conditions

Fixed and Working Capital: Management of Fixed Capital- : Fixed capital refers to investment in long-term assets. It involves allocation of firm's capital to different projects or assets with long-term implications for the business. These decisions are called investment decisions or capital budgeting decisions and affect the growth, profitability and risk of the business in the long run. These long-term assets last for more than one year.

Factors Affecting the Requirement of Fixed Capital

a. Nature of business
b. Scale of operations
c. Choice of techniques
d. Technology upgradation
e. Growth prospectus
f. Diversification
g. Financing alternatives
h. Level of collaboration

Working capital: Working Capital refers to the funds required for the day to day operations of an organization. Apart from the investment in fixed assets every business organization needs to invest in the current assets, which can be converted into cash or cash equivalents within a period of one year.

Factors Affecting the Working Capital Requirement

a. Nature of business
b. Scale of operations
c. Business cycle
d. Seasonal factors
e. Credit allowed
f. Production cycle
g. Credit availed
h. Inflation
i. Level of competition
j. Growth prospects
k. Availability of raw material

Exercise

1. __________ aims at reducing the cost of funds procured, keeping the risk under control and achieving effective deployment of such funds.
   - (a) Market
   - (b) Financial Management
   - (c) Business
   - (d) Activities

2. The primary aim of financial management is to __________ shareholders' wealth.
   - (a) Break- up
   - (b) Mobilise
   - (c) Lower cost
   - (d) Maximise

3. Business finance is needed to
   - (a) Establish a business
   - (b) Diversify
   - (c) Modernise the business
   - (d) All of the above

4. With an __________-in the investment in fixed assets, there is a commensurate increase in the working capital requirement.
   - (a) Increase
   - (b) Decrease
   - (c) No change
   - (d) Proportion

5. From the following statement: choose the right answer

   Statement 1 : Higher amount of debt means higher interest expense in future.

   Statement 2 : the overall financial health of a business is determined by the quality of its financial management.

   Choose the correct option:
   - (a) Both are true
   - (b) Both are false
   - (c) 1 is True , 2 is false
   - (d) 2 is true , 1 is false

6. Financial Management aims at
   - (a) Reducing the cost of funds procured
   - (b) Keeping the risk under control
   - (c) Achieving effective deployment of such funds
   - (d) All of the above

7. A long-term investment decision is also called a __________ decision.
   - (a) Financing
   - (b) Operational
   - (c) Capital Budgeting
   - (d) None of the above

8. __________ decision relates to how the firm's funds are invested in different assets.
   - (a) Investment
   - (b) Financing
   - (c) Budgeting
   - (d) Dividend

9. __________ decision involves identification of various available sources.
   - (a) Investment
   - (b) Financing
   - (c) Budgeting
   - (d) Dividend

10. Justify the statement " : Higher the floatation cost, less attractive the source"
    - (a) Partially true
    - (b) False
    - (c) True
    - (d) None of the above

11. __________ affect the liquidity and profitability of a business.
    - (a) Working capital decision
    - (b) Financing decision
    - (c) Capital budgeting decision
    - (d) none of the above

12. Ashish has two projects A and B (with the same risk involved), with a rate of return of 10 %and 12%, respectively, then under normal circumstance, which one of the two project should be selected
    - (a) Project A
    - (b) Project B
    - (c) Both A and B
    - (d) Neither A nor B

13. The __________ funds refer to the equity capital and the retained earnings.
    - (a) Shareholders
    - (b) Preference
    - (c) Dividend
    - (d) Investment

14. From the following statement: choose the right answer

    Statement 1 : If a business has high fixed operating costs. It must increase fixed financing costs

    Statement 2 : If fixed operating cost is less, more of debt financing should be preferred

    Choose the correct option:
    - (a) Both are true
    - (b) Both are false
    - (c) 1 is True, 2 is false
    - (d) 2 is true, 1 is false

15. __________ is that portion of profit which is distributed to shareholders.
    - (a) Earnings
    - (b) Finances
    - (c) Shares
    - (d) Dividend

16. Which one of the following is not the factor affecting dividend decision?

(a) Amount of earnings

(b) State of capital market

(c) Stability earnings

(d) Cash flow position

17. This decision determines the overall cost of capital and the financial risk of the enterprise,

(a) Dividend decision

(b) Capital budgeting decision

(c) Investment decision

(d) Financing decision

18. ___________ is essentially the preparation of a financial blueprint of an organisation's future operations.

(a) Access to capital market

(b) Contractual constraints

(c) Financial planning

(d) Stock market reaction

19. Which of the following is not considered as importance of financial planning –

(a) Helps in forecasting

(b) Helps in avoiding business shocks

(c) Detailed planned of action is not needed

(d) Links the present with the future .

20. Financial planning provides a link between __________ and financing decisions on a continuous basis.

(a) Investment

(b) Dividend

(c) Budgeting

(d) None of the above

Topic Test – I

1. Guess circumstances under which a company is not likely to declare a higher dividend?

(a) When the earnings of the company are high

(b) When a company has a lucrative forthcoming business opportunity

(c) When the cash flow position of the company is strong

(d) All of the above

2. Assertion (A) : A company follows strict dividend policy when it has easy access to the capital market

Reasoning (R): such a company can raise capital by capital market

Codes:

(a) Both Assertion (A) and Reason (R) are true and Reason (R) is the correct explanation of Assertion (A).

(b) Both Assertion (A) and Reason (R) are true and Reason (R) is not the correct explanation of Assertion (A)

(c) Assertion (A) is true but Reason (R) is False

(d) Assertion (A) is False but Reason (R) is True.

3. ___________ consist of equity share capital, preference share capital and reserves and surpluses or retained earnings.

(a) Owners' funds

(b) Borrowed fund

(c) Invested funds

(d) None of the above

4. ___________ structure refers to the mix between owners and borrowed funds.

(a) Management

(b) Financial

(c) Capital

(d) Debt

5. From the following statement: choose the right answer:

Statement 1 : Debt and equity differ significantly in their cost and riskiness for the firm

Statement 2 : interest paid on debt is a deductible expense for computation of tax liability whereas dividends are paid out of after-tax profit

Choose the correct option:

(a) Both are true

(b) Both are false

(c) 1 is True, 2 is false

(d) 2 is true, 1 is false

6. _______ is cheaper but is more risky for a business because the payment of interest and the return of principal is obligatory for the business.

(a) Equity

(b) Debt

(c) Funds

(d) Capital

7. Precious Earth Ltd. is a company dealing in baby skincare range products. The company is earning high profits but is short on cash, so it has decided to declare less dividends in the current financial year. Identify the factor related to dividend decision being described in the above lines.

(a) amount of earnings

(b) stability of earnings

(c) Cash flow position

(d) stability of dividends

8. This is refer to the mix between owners and borrowed funds.

(a) Capital structure

(b) Earnings

(c) Equity

(d) Dividend

9. The company earns Rs. 0.93 per share if it is unlevered. With debt of Rs. 10 lakh its EPS is Rs. 1.05. With a still higher debt of Rs. 20 lakh, its, EPS rises to Rs. 1.40. Why is the EPS rising with higher debt?

   (a) cost of debt is lower than the return on the earnings

   (b) cost of debt is higher than the return on the earnings

   (c) high rate of interest

   (d) none of the above

10. ____________ refers to increase in profit earned by the equity shareholders due to the presence of fixed financial charges .

   (a) Preference shares

   (b) Trading on equity

   (c) Taxes -earning per share

   (d) Earning before interest

11. Sunil completed his business management from a very good reputed college. His father has restaurant business. Their company has 10 restaurants in united kingdom. As soon as sunil joins the business he decides to take this number to 20 by opening 10 more restaurants in the major cities of London. What do you think will be the fixed capital requirement here?

   (a) The fixed capital requirement would be high.

   (b) The fixed capital requirement would be low

   (c) Will not be effected

   (d) None of the above

Topic Test – II

1. **Assertion (A):** Business finance refers to the money required for carrying out business activities.

   Reasoning (R): financial decision determines the overall cost of capital and the financial risk of the enterprise.

   Codes:

   (a) Both Assertion (A) and Reason (R) are true and Reason (R) is the correct explanation of Assertion (A).

   (b) Both Assertion (A) and Reason (R) are true, but Reason (R) is not the correct explanation of Assertion (A).

   (c) Assertion (A) is true, but Reason (R) is false.

   (d) Assertion (A) is false, but Reason (R) is true.

2. Match the column :

I.	Financial planning	A.	measure how well a firm can pay the interest due on Outstanding debt.
II.	Floatation cost	B.	company incurs when it issues new stock/ bonds.
III.	Interest coverage ratio	C.	preparation of a financial blueprint of an organisation's future operations

   Choose the correct option:

   (a) I-C, II-B, III-A

   (b) II-A, I-C, III-B

   (c) I-A, II-B, III-C

   (d) III-A, II-C, III-B

3. Name the decision that affects the liquidity as well as profitability of a business.

   (a) Capital budgeting

   (b) Working capital

   (c) Financing

   (d) Dividend

4. Capital structure shows ______________.

   (a) Interest coverage ratio

   (b) Gaining ratio

   (c) Debt-equity ratio

   (d) Current ratio

5. Which of the following is not a factor affecting working capital requirement

   (a) Scale of operations

   (b) Seasonal factors

   (c) Credit allowed

   (d) Raw materials

6. ______________ are those payment obligations which are due for payment within one year.

   (a) Current liabilities

   (b) Expenses

   (c) Equivalents

   (d) Advances

7. This decision relates to how the firm's funds are invested in different assets,

   (a) Investment decision

   (b) Financing decision

   (c) Dividend decision

   (d) None of the above

8. A company is growing by leaps and bounds. Every year it is opening new branches in the major cities of the country. There are chances that in a few years to come it will be the market leader in its industry. Newspapers appreciate the steps taken by the management. However in the field of financial decisions the company takes a defensive stand. Every year it declares less than expected dividend for the shareholders. Identify the factors involved in the following dividend decisions

   (a) Growth opportunities.(b) Taxation policy.

   (c) Cash flow position.   (d) Stability of dividends.

9. Justify statement as " Investment decision can be long term or short-term".

   (a) False

   (b) True

   (c) Partially false

   (d) None of the above

10. __________ is that portion of profit which is distributed to shareholders.

   (a) Dividend   (b) Earnings

   (c) Debt   (d) Investment

11. **Assertion (A):** The objective of financial planning is to ensure that enough funds are available at right time.

   Reasoning (R): Dividend is that portion of profit which is distributed to shareholders.

   Codes:

   (a) Both Assertion (A) and Reason (R) are true and Reason (R) is the correct explanation of Assertion (A).

   (b) Both Assertion (A) and Reason (R) are true, but Reason (R) is not the correct explanation of Assertion (A).

   (c) Assertion (A) is true, but Reason (R) is false.

   (d) Assertion (A) is false, but Reason (R) is true.

Answers

1. (b)	**2.** (d)	**3.** (d)	**4.** (a)	**5.** (a)	**6.** (d)	**7.** (c)	**8.** (a)	**9.** (b)	**10.** (c)
11. (a)	**12.** (b)	**13.** (a)	**14.** (d)	**15.** (d)	**16.** (b)	**17.** (d)	**18.** (c)	**19.** (c)	**20.** (a)

Topic – I

1. (b)	**2.** b	**3.** (a)	**4.** (c)	**5.** (a)	**6.** (c)	**7.** (c)	**8.** (a)	**9.** (a)	**10.** (b)
11. (a)									

Topic – II

1. (b)	**2.** (a)	**3.** (b)	**4.** (c)	**5.** (d)	**6.** (a)	**7.** (a)	**8.** (a)	**9.** (b)	**10.** (a)
11. (b)									

CHAPTER 10

Financial Markets

Financial market is a link between savers and the borrowers; a financial market helps to establish a link between savers and the investors by mobilising funds between them.

Functions of Financial Market

1. **Mobilization of savings:** It is an allocative function of financial market that it facilitates transfer of people's saving to investors.

2. **Price fixation:** price is determined from the forces of demand and supply. The interaction between demand and supply helps to establish a price for financial asset.

3. **Provides liquidity to financial assets:** shareholders can sell their share easily through mechanism of financial market.

4. **Reduce the cost of transactions:** provides valuable information to buyers and sellers of financial assets & helps in saving time money and efforts.

Money Market

The money market is a market for short term funds which deals in monetary assets whose period of maturity is up to one year. It is a market where low risk, unsecured and short term debt instruments that are highly liquid are issued and actively traded everyday. It enables the raising of short-term funds for meeting the temporary shortages of cash and obligations and the temporary deployment of excess funds for earning returns.

Instruments of Money Market

i. **Call money:** is used by banks, insurance company & financial companies. Under this bank lends cash for one or two days to other bank that are in shortage of cash. It is repayable on demand with maturity period of 1 to 15 days.

ii. **Treasury Bills:** are issued by RBI on behalf of the govt. of India for a period of 14 to 364 days. These bills are very popular as no interest is paid on these bills. Issued at a minimum amount of Rs. 25000 and are also called Zero coupon Bond.

iii. **Trade Bills:** are drawn by one business firm on other business firm, normal duration is 90 days. Such bills are freely transferable and can be easily discounted from banks.

iv. **Commercial paper:** is issued by the public/private sector companies with good reputation. It is an unsecured promissory note issued with fixed maturity period up to 12 months. It provides short term funds for seasonal & working capital needs.

v. **Certificate of Deposits:** are unsecured, short term instruments issued by commercial banks & financial institutions during periods of tight liquidity when deposits growth of banks is slow & demand of credit is high.

vi. **Capital market:** The term capital market refers to facilities and institutional arrangements through which long-term funds, both debt and equity are raised and invested. It consists of a series of channels through which savings of the community are made available for industrial and commercial enterprises and for the public in general. The instruments used in capital markets are equity, preference shares and debentures.

1. **Primary Market:** primary market is the market, in which a security is sold for the first time. The securities issued are equity shares, preference shares, & Debentures.

Methods of issuing Securities in Primary Market

i. **Initial public offer:** If a company wants to issue capital to the public through the online system of the stock exchange has to enter in an agreement with a stock exchange, this is called an initial public offer.

ii. **Offer through prospectus:** This involves inviting subscription from the public through issue of prospectus. A prospectus is a document inviting deposits from the public for the subscription of any shares or debentures.

iii. **Offer for sale:** The securities are not issued directly to the public but are offered to the public for sale through stock brokers.

iv. **Private placement:** Under this method securities are allotted to institutional investors and some selected individuals.

v. **Right Issue:** this is a special facility given to existing shareholders to subscribe to a new issue of shares according to the terms & conditions of the company.

2. **Secondary Market:** The secondary market is also known as the stock market or stock exchange. It is a market for the purchase and sale of existing securities. It helps existing investors to disinvest and fresh investors to enter the market. It also provides liquidity and marketability to existing securities

Stock exchange: A stock exchange is an institution which provides a platform for buying and selling of existing securities. As a market, the stock exchange facilitates the exchange of a security (share, debenture etc.) into money and vice versa. According to Securities Contracts (Regulation) Act 1956, stock exchange means any body of individuals, whether incorporated or not, constituted for the purpose of assisting, regulating or controlling the business of buying and selling or dealing in securities.

Functions of Stock Exchange

1. Providing Liquidity and Marketability to Existing Securities
2. Pricing of Securities
3. Safety of Transaction
4. Spreading of Equity Cult
5. Providing Scope for Speculation
6. Contributes to Economic Growth

Trading Procedure on a Stock Exchange

1. **Selection of Broker:** in order to trade on a Stock Exchange first a broker is selected who should be a member of stock exchange as they can only trade on the stock exchange.
2. **Placing the order:** After selecting a broker, the investors specify the type and number of securities they want to buy or sell.
3. **Executing the order:** The broker will buy or sell the securities as per the instructions of the investor.
4. **Settlement:** Transactions on a stock exchange may be carried out on either cash basis or carry over basis . The time period for which the transactions are carried forward is referred to as accounts which vary from a fortnight to a month. All transactions made during one account are to be settled by payment for purchases and by delivery of share certificates, which is a proof of ownership of securities by an individual.

Dematerialisation and Depositories: All trading in securities is now done through computer terminals. Since all systems are computerised, buying and selling of securities are settled through an electronic book entry form. This is mainly done to eliminate problems like theft, fake/forged transfers, transfer delays and paperwork associated with share certificates or debentures held in physical form.

Demat Account

Demat (Dematerialized) account refers to an account which an Indian citizen must open with the depository participant (banks, stockbrokers) to trade in listed securities in electronic form. The securities are held in the electronic form by a depository

Securities and Exchange Board of India (SEBI)

SEBI was established by Government of India on 12 April 1988 as an interim administrative body to promote orderly and healthy growth of securities market and for investor protection. It was given a statutory status on 30 January 1992 through an ordinance which was later replaced by an Act of Parliament known as the SEBI Act, 1992. It seeks to protect the interest of investors in new and second hand securities.

Objectives of SEBI

1. Protection of Investors
2. Steady Flow of Savings
3. Control over Brokers
4. Transparency in transactions
5. Fair Practices by Issuers

Functions of SEBI

1. **Regulating functions:**
   (a) Registration of brokers and sub brokers and other players in the market.
   (b) Registration of collective investment schemes and Mutual Funds.
   (c) Regulation of stock brokers, portfolio exchanges, underwriters and merchant bankers and the business in stock exchanges and any other securities market.
   (d) Regulation of takeover bids by companies.
   (e) Calling for information by undertaking inspection, conducting enquiries and audits of stock exchanges and intermediaries.
   (f) Levying fee or other charges for carrying out the purposes of the Act.

2. **Developmental functions:**
   a) Training of intermediaries of the securities market.
   b) Conducting research and publishing information useful to all market participants.
   c) Undertaking measures to develop the capital markets by adapting a flexible approach.

3. **Protective functions:-**
   a) Controlling insider trading and imposing penalties for such practices.
   b) Undertaking steps for investor protection.
   c) Promotion of fair practices and code of conduct in securities market

Exercise

1. Which of the following is not the function of financial market

(a) Facilitating price discovery

(b) Providing liquidity to financial assets

(c) Reducing the cost of transactions.

(d) Scarce resources

2. Name the process by which allocation of funds is done

(a) Financial market

(b) Financial intermediation

(c) Financial management

(d) IPO

3. _________________ facilitates the transfer of savings from savers to investors.

(a) Financial markets   (b) Banks

(c) Shareholders   (d) Top management

4. Which one of the following is a money market instrument?

(a) Unit of mutual fund   (b) Debenture

(c) Bond   (d) Treasury bill

5. The _______________ market is a market for short term funds which deals in monetary assets whose period of maturity is upto one year.

(a) Capital   (b) Working – capital

(c) Money   (d) Temporary

6. State which of the following statement is true

Statement I: Financial markets provide valuable information about securities being traded in the market

Statement II: money market has specific physical locations.

Choose the correct option:

(a) Statement I is correct and II is wrong.   (b) Statement II is correct and I is wrong.

(c) Both the statements are correct.   (d) Both the statements are incorrect.

7. When funds raised through commercial paper used to meet the floatation costs. This is known as ___________.

(a) Bridge Financing   (b) Minimum amount

(c) Promissory note   (d) Short term financing

8. Secondary market is in the form of:

(a) Stock exchange.   (b) Money market

(c) New issue market.   (d) Commercial exchange

9. They are also called Zero Coupon Bonds issued by the Reserve Bank of India on behalf of the Central Government to meet its short-term requirement of funds.

(a) Shares   (b) Debentures

(c) Treasury bill   (d) Bonds

10. _______________ usually has a maturity period of 15 days to one year.

(a) Calm money   (b) Treasury bill

(c) Bonds   (d) Commercial paper

11. These days, the development of a country is also judged by its system of transferring finance from the sector where it is in surplus to the sector where it is needed most. To give strength to the economy, SEBI is undertaking measures to develop the capital market. In addition to this there is another market in which unsecured and short-term debt instruments are actively traded everyday. These markets together help the savers and investors in directing the available funds into their most productive investment opportunity. Name the function being performed by the market in the above case.

(a) Price discovery

(b) Mobilisation of Savings

(c) Reducing the cost of transactions

(d) Liquidity

12. Which of the following statements is not true with regard to Call money?

(a) It is short-term finance repayable on demand.

(b) Its maturity period ranges from one day to fifteen days.

(c) There is a direct relationship between call rates and other short-term money market instruments.

(d) It is used for inter-bank transactions.

13. The main instruments traded in the capital market are

(a) Equity shares   (b) Preference shares

(c) Bonds   (d) All of the above

14. State which of the following statement is true

Statement I: money market deals in medium and long term securities

Statement II: Capital market instruments have a maximum tenure of one year, and may even be issued for a single day

Choose the correct option:

(a) Statement I is correct and II is wrong.

(b) Statement II is correct and I is wrong.

(c) Both the statements are correct

(d) Both the statements are incorrect

15. Sameer's Grandfather has gifted him the shares of a large cement company with which he had been working. The securities were in physical form. He already has a bank account and does not possess any other forms of securities.

He wished to sell the shares and approached a registered broker for the purpose. Mention one mandatory detail which he will have to provide with the broker.

(a) DEMAT Account

(b) Bank Account

(c) Permanent Account Number

(d) Adhaar card

16. Which of the following statements is not true with regard to Treasury bills?

(a) Issued in the form of a promissory note.

(b) Are highly liquid and have assured yield

(c) Carry high risk of default.

(d) Are available for a minimum amount of Rs, 25,000 and in multiples thereof

17. ______ is a market for short-term funds which deals in monetary assets whose period of maturity is up to one year.

(a) Primary market   (b) Secondary market

(c) Capital market   (d) Money market

18. Assertion (A): Primary Market promotes capital formation directly.

Reasoning (R): A company can raise capital through the primary market in the form of equity shares, debentures, loans, etc.

Codes:

(a) Both Assertion (A) and Reason (R) are true and Reason (R) is the correct explanation of Assertion (A).

(b) Both Assertion (A) and Reason (R) are true and Reason (R) is not the correct explanation of Assertion (A).

(c) Assertion (A) is true but Reason (R) is False.

(d) Assertion (A) is False but Reason (R) is True.

19. Sally Ltd. issued prospectus for the subscription of its shares for Rs. 400 crores in 2019. The issue was oversubscribed by 10 times. The company issued shares to all the applicants on pro-rata basis. Later SEBI inspected the prospectus and found some misleading statement about the management of the company in it. SEBI imposed a penalty of Rs. 3 crores and banned its three executive directors for dealing in securities market for three years. Identify the function and its type performed by SEBI in the above case.

(a) Protective function   (b) Development function

(c) Regulatory function   (d) All of the above

20. Under this method of floatation in primary market, a subscription is invited from general public to invest in the securities of a company through the issue of advertisement.

(a) Private placement

(b) Offer through prospectus

(c) Offer for sale

(d) None of the above

Topic Test – I

1. State which of the following statement is true

Statement I: BSE Ltd. was established in 1875.

Statement II: The OTCEI is a company incorporated under the Companies Act 1956

Choose the correct option:

(a) Statement I is correct and II is wrong.

(b) Statement II is correct and I is wrong.

(c) Both the statements are correct.

(d) Both the statements are incorrect.

2. Financial markets are classified on the basis of the __________ of financial instruments traded in them;

(a) Maturity   (b) Substitutes

(c) Temporary   (d) Permanent

3. Which of the following statements is not true with regard to capital market?

(a) The funds are raised for a long period of time.

(b) Both debt and equity funds can be raised

(c) It is classified into three types.

(d) All of the above.

4. ____________ are highly liquid and have assured yield and negligible risk of default.

(a) Commercial paper   (b) Treasury bill

(c) Call money   (d) Bonds

5. These days, the development of a country is also judged by its system of transferring finance from the sector where it is in surplus to the sector where it is needed most. To give strength to the economy, SEBI is undertaking measures to develop the capital market. In addition to this there is another market in which unsecured and short-term debt instruments are actively traded everyday. These markets together help the savers and investors in directing the available funds into their most productive investment opportunity. Name the function being performed by the market in the above case.

(a) Facilitating Price Discovery

(b) Reducing the Cost of Transactions

(c) Mobilisation of funds

(d) Providing liquidity

6. Suppose Mr. Sharma an investor purchases a 91 days Treasury bill with a face value of Rs. 2,00,000 for Rs. 1,92,000. By holding the bill until the maturity date, the investor receives Rs. 2,00,000. What is the amount of interest received by him?

    (a) Rs. 20,000 (b) Rs. 8000

    (c) Rs. 1,00,000 (d) Rs. 2,08,000

7. **Assertion (A):** Treasury Bills are considered negotiable instruments.

    Reasoning (R): A Treasury Bill can be transferred to another person, so it is payable "to order."

    Codes:

    (a) Both Assertion (A) and Reason (R) are true and Reason (R) is the correct explanation of Assertion (A).

    (b) Both Assertion (A) and Reason (R) are true and Reason (R) is not the correct explanation of Assertion(A).

    (c) Assertion(A) is true but Reason (R) is False.

    (d) Assertion (A) is False but Reason (R) is True.

8. The capital market consists of

    (a) Development banks (b) Commercial banks

    (c) Stock exchanges (d) All of the above

9. Which of the following is not an advantage of electronic trading systems:

    (a) It ensures transparency

    (b) It increases efficiency of information

    (c) A single trading platform has been provided

    (d) It decreases the efficiency of operations

10. Process of holding securities in an electronic form is called ______________

    (a) Dematerialisation (b) Depository

    (c) Settlement cycle (d) IPO's

11. Match the column:

    I. OTC Market   A. conform to international standards

    II. SEBI   B. provides a trading platform to smaller and less liquid companies

    III. BSE   C. aims to stimulate competition and encourage innovation

    Choose the correct option:

    (a) I-B, II-C, III-A

    (b) II-A, I-C, III-B

    (c) III-A, II-B, I-C

    (d) I-A, II-B, III-C

Topic Test – II

1. Shantanu's Grandfather who, was unwell, called him and gave him a gift packet. Shantanu opened the packet and saw many crumpled share certificates inside. His grandfather told him that they had been left behind by his late grandfather. As no trading is now done in physical form, Shantanu wants to know the process by adopting which he is in a position to deal with these certificates. Identify and state the process.

    (a) Depositories (b) Settlement cycle

    (c) Dematerialization (d) Bridge financing

2. **Assertion (A):** Commercial Paper is used for Bridge Financing.

    Reasoning (R):- Funds raised through commercial paper are used to meet the floatation costs.

    Codes:

    (a) Both Assertion (A) and Reason (R) are true and Reason (R) is the correct explanation of Assertion (A).

    (b) Both Assertion (A) and Reason (R) are true and Reason (R) is not the correct explanation of Assertion (A).

    (c) Assertion (A) is true but Reason (R) is False.

    (d) Assertion (A) is False but Reason (R) is True.

3. State which of the following statement is true

    Statement I: The money market is a market for short term funds.

    Statement II: Financial markets lacks in providing valuable information about securities being traded in the market.

    Choose the correct option:

    (a) Statement I is correct and II is wrong.

    (b) Statement II is correct and I is wrong.

    (c) Both the statements are correct.

    (d) Both the statements are incorrect.

4. ___________is a source of financing to meet very short-term fund requirements of commercial banks with a provision of renewal.

    (a) Treasury Bill

    (b) Commercial Paper

    (c) Certificate of Deposit

    (d) Call Money

5. The SEBI was given a statutory status on 30th January ___________through an ordinance.

    (a) 1991 (b) 1992

    (c) 1993 (d) 1995

6. Army sand Ltd. is a large creditworthy company that manufactures coaches for the Indian Railways. It now wants to export these coaches to other countries and decides to invest in new hi-tech machines. Since the investment is large, it requires long-term finance. It decides to raise funds by issuing equity shares. The issue of equity shares involves huge floatation cost. To meet the expenses of floatation cost, the company decides to tap the money market. Name the money-market instrument the company can use for the above purpose.

   (a) Commercial Papers (b) Treasury bills

   (c) Call money   (d) Demat account

7. Potter Securities Pvt. Ltd" was established to deal in securities. It was registered as a stock broker with National Stock Exchange (NSE) and Bombay Stock Exchange (BSE) to trade in securities listed at these exchanges. It is also a depository participant with CDSL and NSDL. In the first three years, it developed its business successfully. After that the composition of Board of Directors changed. Some customers complained to the customer care centre of the company that shares purchased by them and for which the payment has been duly made, were not transferred to their D'mat Accounts by "Potter securities Pvt. Ltd". The executive of customer care centre promised the aggrieved customers that their shares will be transferred to their respective D'mat Accounts very soon. But the company delayed the matter and didn't transfer the shares of the customers to their D'mat Accounts. This eroded investors confidence and multiplied, their grievances. Name the Apex statutory body of capital market to whom customer can complain to redress their grievances.

   (a) SEBI   (b) UNICEF

   (c) WHO   (d) IPO's

8. Secondary market is in the form of

   (a) Stock exchange.

   (b) Money market.

   (c) New issue market.

   (d) Commercial exchange.

9. Match the correct answer:

I.	Regulatory Functions	A.	Promotion of fair practices and code of conduct in securities market.
II.	Development Functions	B.	Registration of collective investment schemes and Mutual Funds.
III.	Protective Functions	C.	Training of intermediaries of the securities market.

   Choose the correct option:

   (a) II-B, III-A, I-C   (b) II-C, I-B, II-A

   (c) I-C, II-B, III-A   (d) I-A, II-B, III-C

10. _______ is the institution which provides a platform for trading of existing securities having long-term maturity.

    (a) SEBI   (b) WTO

    (c) Stock exchange   (d) RBI

11. A company can raise capital through the primary market in the form of

    (a) Equity shares   (b) Preference shares

    (c) Debentures   (d) All of the above

Answers

1. (d)	**2.** (b)	**3.** (a)	**4.** (d)	**5.** (c)	**6.** (a)	**7.** (a)	**8.** (a)	**9.** (c)	**10.** (d)
11. (b)	**12.** (c)	**13.** (d)	**14.** (d)	**15.** (c)	**16.** (c)	**17.** (d)	**18.** (b)	**19.** (a)	**20.** (b)

Topic – I

1. (c)	**2.** (a)	**3.** (c)	**4.** (b)	**5.** (c)	**6.** (b)	**7.** (a)	**8.** (d)	**9.** (d)	**10.** (a)
11. (a)									

Topic – II

1. (c)	**2.** (a)	**3.** (a)	**4.** (d)	**5.** (b)	**6.** (a)	**7.** (a)	**8.** (a)	**9.** (b)	**10.** (c)
11. (d)									

CHAPTER 11

Marketing

SUMMARY

Market can be defined where deal is accomplished between buyers sellers it may be at particular place, letter or through the medium of internet.

Marketing involves a process of satisfying the needs of both the buyers & sellers so that all the transactions between buyers & sellers take place voluntary.

Features of marketing

1. **Needs and Wants:** The process of marketing helps individuals and groups in obtaining what they need and want. A need is a state of felt deprivation or feeling of being deprived of something. Wants, on the other hand, are culturally defined objects that are potential satisfiers of needs.

2. **Creating a marketing offering:** Market offering refers to a complete offer for a product or service, having given features like size, quality, taste, etc; at a certain price; available at a given outlet or location and so on.

3. **Customer value:** The process of marketing facilitates exchange of products and services between the buyers and the sellers.

4. **Exchange Mechanism:** The process of marketing involves exchange of products and services for money or something considered valuable by the people.

Marketing Management

Marketing management refers to planning, organising, directing and control of the activities which facilitate exchange of goods and services between producers and consumers or users of products and services. Thus the focus of marketing management is on achieving desired exchange outcomes with the target markets. Marketing management involves performance of various functions such as analysing and planning the marketing activities, implementing marketing plans and setting control mechanism. These functions are to be performed in such a way that organisation's objectives are achieved at the minimum cost

Concept of marketing management

1. **Product concept:** those companies who believe in this philosophy are of the opinion that if the quality of goods and services is of good standard the customers are attracted.

2. **Production concept:** producer who aims at maximizing their sale by selling their product at different places adopts procedures of production at large scale.

3. **Selling concept:** under this concept the firms believe that customers will buy a product when they are convinced to buy it by some selling or promotional method and thus make use of advertising, etc.

4. **Marketing concept:** this concept pays attention to the needs of customers. The firm believes that customer satisfaction is the pre-condition in achieving firm's goals.

Selling

Focuses on the needs of seller. Those activities which are undertaken to secure the sale or distribution of goods among the customers.

Functions of Marketing

1. **Gathering & Analyzing Market Information:** this is necessary to identify the needs of the customers & take various decisions for the successful marketing.

2. **Market planning:** New important area of work of a marketer is to develop suitable marketing plans so that marketing objectives of the organization can be achieved.

3. **Product Designing & Development:** Design of the product contributes to making the product attractive to the target customers.

4. **Standardization & Grading:** Standardisation refers to producing goods of predetermined specifications, which helps in achieving uniformity and consistency in the output E.g. ISI Mark etc.

   - Grading Is the process of classification of products into different groups, based on some of its important characteristics such as quality, size, etc

5. **Packaging & Labelling:** Packaging' refers to designing and developing a package for a product.

   - It protects the products from damage , risks of spoilage, breakage and leakage. It also makes buying convenient for customers and serves as a promotional tool. Labelling refers to designing a label to be put on the package. It may vary from a simple tag to complex graphics.

6. **Branding:** It helps in differentiation of the product, builds customer loyalty and promote its sale.

   - Important decision area is branding strategy, whether each product will have a separate brand name or the same brand name to be used for all products.

7. **Customer Support Services**: A very important function of the marketing management relates to developing customer support services such as after sales services, handling customer complaints and adjustments, procuring credit services, maintenance services, technical services and consumer information.

8. **Pricing of products:** Price of product refers to the amount of money customers have to pay to obtain a product.

   - It is an important factor in the success/ failure of a product.

   - Demand for a product/ service is related to its price, so price should be fixed after analysing all the factors determining the price of the product.

9. **Promotion:** Promotion of products and services involves informing the customers about the firm's product, its features, etc. and persuading them to buy the products.

   - Methods of promotion are advertising, Personal Selling, Publicity and Sales Promotion.

10. **Physical Distribution:** The two major decision areas under this function include (a) decision regarding channels of distribution or the marketing intermediaries (like wholesalers , retailers) to be used and (b) physical movement of the product from where it is produced to a place where it is required by the customers for their consumption or use.

11. **Transportation:** Transportation means physical movement of goods from one place to the other. • Various factors like nature of the product, cost, location of target market etc. should be considered in choosing the mode of transport.

12. **Storage or Warehousing:** In the process of marketing, the function of storage is performed by different agencies such as manufacturers, wholesalers and retailers.

Marketing Mix

Involves creating a market offering to satisfy the needs and wants of the customer. The set of marketing tools that a firm uses to pursue its marketing objectives in the target market is described as Marketing Mix.

Elements of Marketing Mix

1. **Product:** means goods & services or anything of value which is offered to the market for exchange.

2. **Price:** is the amount of money customers have to pay to obtain the product.

3. **Place:** include activities that make firm products available to the target customers.

4. **Promotion:** of products & services include activities that communicate availability, features merits, etc.

Products

A buyer buys a product or service for what it does for her or the benefit it provides to her.

Classification of Products :- Products may broadly be classified into two categories —

1. **Consumers' products:** Products, which are purchased by the ultimate consumers or users for satisfying their personal needs and desires are referred to as consumer products. They can be categorised as :-

   a) **Convenience Products:** Those consumer products, which are purchased frequently, for immediate use are referred to as convenience goods. Medicines, newspaper, stationery items, toothpaste. etc.

   b) **Shopping Products:** Shopping products are those goods, in which buyers devote considerable time, to compare the quality, price, style, suitability, etc., at several stores, before making final purchase. E.g. electronic goods, vehicles etc.

   c) **Specialty Products:** Specialty products are those goods which have certain special features because of which people make special efforts in their purchase. E.g. art work, antiques etc.

Durability of Products:

a) **Non-durable Products:** The consumer products, which are consumed in a short span of time. E.g. milk, soap, stationary etc.

b) **Durable Products:** Those tangible products which normally survive many uses, for e.g. refrigerator, radio, bicycle etc.

c) **Services:** Services are intangible, it means those activities, benefits or satisfactions, which are offered for sale.

Industrial products are those products, which are used as inputs in producing other products. The examples of such products are raw materials, engines, lubricants, machines, tools, etc. They can be classified as :-

a) **Materials and parts:** These include goods that enter the manufacture's products completely.

b) **Capital Items:** These are such goods that are used in the production of finished goods.

c) **Supplies and Business Services:** These are short lasting goods and services that facilitate developing or managing the finished product.

Branding

Branding implies **giving a unique name, sign, symbol or term for the identification of a product**

The various terms relating to branding are as follows:

1. **Brand:** A brand is a name, term, sign, symbol, design or some combination of them, used to identify the products — goods or services of one seller or group of sellers and to differentiate them from those of the competitors.

2. **Brand Name:** That part of a brand, which can be spoken, is called a brand name. In other words, brand name is the verbal component of a brand

3. **Brand Mark:** That part of a brand which can be recognised but which is not utterable is called brand mark. It appears in the form of a symbol, design, distinct colour scheme or lettering.

4. **Trade Mark:** A brand or part of a brand that is given legal protection is called trademark.

Characteristics of a good brand name:

1. should be short & simple
2. Should be easily pronounce
3. Should be unique & distinctive

Packaging

Packaging refers to the act of designing and producing the container or wrapper of a product. It plays a very important role in the marketing success or failure of many products, particularly the consumer non-durable products.

Levels of Packaging: There can be three different levels of packaging.

1. **Primary Package:** It refers to the product's immediate container. E.g :- a match box , a wrapper of soap.

2. **Secondary Packaging:** It refers to additional layers of protection that are kept till the product is ready for use, e.g., a tube of shaving cream usually comes in a card board box.

3. **Transportation Packaging:** It refers to further packaging components necessary for storage, identification or transportation.

Packaging Functions:

1. Product protection
2. Product identification
3. Facilitating Use of the Product:
4. Product promotion

Labelling

Labelling means **attaching a piece of paper, or a printed material or an unprinted one to display the contents of the product** such as the name of the manufacturer, price of the product, place of manufacturing and all such things that can be beneficial to the consumers.

Functions of labelling:

i. Identify the product
ii. Describe the product and its contents
iii. Grading of products
iv. Helps in promotion of products
v. Providing information required by law

Pricing

Sum of the values that consumers exchange for the benefit of having or using the product. Price may therefore be defined as the amount of money paid by a buyer (or received by a seller) in consideration of the purchase of a product or a service.

Factors affecting Price Determination:

i. Product cost
ii. The utility and demand
iii. Extent of competition in the market
iv. Government and legal regulations
v. Pricing objectives
vi. Marketing method used

Physical Distribution

It covers all the activities required to physically move goods from manufacturers to the customers. A set of decisions needs to be taken to make the product available to customers for purchase and consumption.

- The marketer needs to make sure that the product is available at the right quantity, at the right time and at the right place.

Components of Physical Distribution:

1. Order processing
2. Transportation
3. Warehousing
4. Inventory control

Promotion

Promotion refers to the use of communication with the twin objective of informing potential customers about a product and persuading them to buy it. It is an important element of marketing mix by which marketers makes use of various tools of communication to encourage exchange of goods and services in the market.

Promotion Mix: refers to combination of promotional tools used by an organization to achieve its communication objective. Various tools of communication are used by the marketers to inform and persuade customers about their firm's products. These include: (i) Advertising, (ii) Personal Selling, (iii) Sales Promotion, and (iv) Publicity

Advertising: any paid form of non-personal presentation & promotion of ideas, goods & services of an identified sponsor".

Merits of advertising:

i.   Mass Reach

ii. Enhancing Customer Satisfaction and Confidence

iii. Expressiveness

iv. Economy

Objections to Advertising:

i.   Adds to cost

ii. Undermines social values

iii. Confuses the buyer

iv. Encourage sale of inferior products

Personal selling: involves oral presentation of message in the form of conversation with one or more prospective customers for the purpose of making sales.

Features of the Personal Selling:

1. Personal contact is established under personal selling.

2. Development of relationship with the prospective customers which are important in making sale.

3. Oral conversation.

4. Quick solution of queries

Importance of Personal Selling

1. maximum satisfaction to consumers

2. Effective tool of sale

3. Knowledge of proposed buyers

4. More effective

Sales promotion: refers to short term incentives, which are designed to encourage the buyers to make immediate purchase of a product or service. It includes rebates, discount, refunds, product combination, lucky draw, etc.

Merits of Sales Promotion:

1. Attention value

2. Useful in new product launch

3. Synergy in Total Promotional Efforts

Limitations of sales promotion:

1. Reflect crisis

2. Spoils product image

Commonly used sales Promotion activities:

1. Rebate

2. Discount

3. Refunds

4. Product combination

5. Quantity gift

6. Lucky draw

Public Relations

Public relations covers a wide range of tactics and is usually involved in providing information to independent media sources in the hope of gaining favorable coverage. It also involves a mix of promoting specific products, services and events and promoting the overall brand of an organization, which is an ongoing tact.

Role of Public Relations:

i.   Publicity

ii. Press release

iii. Corporate communication

iv. Lobbying

v.   Counselling

Exercise

1. A ___________ is a state of felt deprivation or feeling of being deprived of something.
   - (a) Need
   - (b) Want
   - (c) Product
   - (d) Selling

2. "Availability and affordability of the product were considered to be the key to the success of a firm." Identify the concept of marketing management highlighted by this statement.
   - (a) Production concept
   - (b) Product Concept
   - (c) Societal concept
   - (d) Marketing Concept

3. With which element is exchange mechanism related?
   - (a) Publicity
   - (b) Marketing
   - (c) Advertising
   - (d) Branding

4. State which of the following statement is true

   Statement I: Advertising is an impersonal form of communication

   Statement II: Advertising lacks direct feedback.

   Choose the correct option:
   - (a) Statement I is correct and II is wrong
   - (b) Statement II is correct and I is wrong
   - (c) Both the statements are correct
   - (d) Both the statements are incorrect

5. ___________ refers to a complete offer for a product or service, having given features like size, quality, taste, etc; at a certain price; available at a given outlet or location, etc.
   - (a) Selling
   - (b) Market offering
   - (c) Exchange
   - (d) facilities

6. A person feeling hungry may get food by offering to give money or some other product or service in return to someone who is willing to accept the same for food. The important feature of marketing illustrated above is:
   - (a) Exchange mechanism
   - (b) Customer value
   - (c) Creating a market offering
   - (d) Needs and wants

7. A ___________ refers to any person who takes more active part in the process of exchange.
   - (a) Marketing
   - (b) Marketer
   - (c) Buyer
   - (d) Seller

8. **Assertion (A):** According to Marketing Concepts, products are bought because of their quality and other features.

   Reasoning (R): Marketing orientation implies that focus on satisfaction of customer's needs is the key to the success of any organisation in the market

   Codes:
   - (a) Both Assertion (A) and Reason (R) are true and Reason (R) is the correct explanation of Assertion (A).
   - (b) Both Assertion (A) and Reason (R) are true and Reason (R) is not the correct explanation of Assertion (A).
   - (c) Assertion (A) is true but Reason (R) is False.
   - (d) Assertion (A) is False but Reason (R) is true.

9. Which of the following is not a function of marketing:
   - (a) Gathering and Analysing Market Information
   - (b) Product Designing and Development
   - (c) Starting point
   - (d) Packaging and Labelling

10. Which one of the following promotion tools has mass reach?
    - (a) Advertising
    - (b) Personal selling
    - (c) Sales promotion
    - (d) Public relations

11. Sunil took his niece, Aarohi for shopping to 'Lauren ' to buy her a dress on the occasion of her birthday. She was delighted when on payment for the dress she got a discount voucher to get 20% off for a meal of Rs. 500 or above at a famous eating joint.

    Identify the technique of sales promotion used by the company in the above situation.
    - (a) Discount
    - (b) Lucky Draw
    - (c) Usable Benefit
    - (d) Quantity Gift

12. _________ ensures that products reach the ultimate customers from the manufacturers.
    - (a) Selling
    - (b) Marketing
    - (c) Physical distribution
    - (d) Sales promotion

13. State which of the following statement is true

    Statement I: marketing is a physical process

    Statement II: The process of marketing works through the exchange mechanism.

    Choose the correct option:
    - (a) Statement I is correct and II is wrong
    - (b) Statement II is correct and I is wrong
    - (c) Both the statements are correct
    - (d) Both the statements are incorrect

14. ___________ refers to planning, organising, directing and control of the activities which facilitate exchange of goods and services between producers and consumers or users of products and services.

(a) Exchange

(b) Marketer

(c) marketing management

(d) None of the above

15. __________ of products and services involves informing the customers about the firm's product, its features, etc., and persuading them to purchase these products.

(a) Promotion   (b) Pricing of Product

(c) Branding   (d) Labeling

16. __________ means goods or services or 'anything of value', which is offered to the market for sale.

(a) Transportation   (b) Manufacturing

(c) Product   (d) Price

17. ______ products are those consumer goods where buyers devote considerable time, to compare the quality, price, style, suitability, etc., before making final purchase.

(a) Convenience   (b) Speciality

(c) Shopping   (d) Industrial

18. Volvo , a marketer of cars having 40 % of the current market share of the country aims at increasing the market share to 70% in next few years. For achieving this objective the manager of the company specified the action programme covering various aspects. Identify the function of marketing discussed above:

(a) Customer support services

(b) Gathering and Analysing market information

(c) Product designing and development

(d) Marketing Planning

19. The marketing management philosophy which is based on the premise that any activity which satisfies human needs but does not pay attention to the ethical and ecological aspects of marketing cannot be justified is known as:

(a) Marketing concept

(b) Societal marketing concept

(c) Production concept

(d) Product concept

20. Shivanya Hotel in kerela was facing a problem of low demand for its rooms due to off¬season. The Managing Director (MD) of the hotel, Mr. Sharma was very worried. He called upon the marketing Manager, Mr. Kapoor for his advice. He suggested that the hotel should announce an offer of '3 Days and 2 nights hotel stay package' with free breakfast and one-day visit to varkala beach and waterfall. The MD liked the suggestion very much. Identify the promotional tool which can be used by the hotel through which large number of tourists all over the country and abroad can be reached, informed and persuaded to use the incentive.

(a) Advertising   (b) Personal selling

(c) Discount coupons   (d) Personal selling

21. __________ involves oral presentation of message in the form of conversation with one or more prospective customers for the purpose of making sales.

(a) Discounts   (b) Personal selling

(c) Advertisement   (d) Social values

Topic Test – I

1. Assertion (A): According to Marketing Concepts, products are bought because of their quality and other features.

Reasoning (R): The marketing concept aims to find out the needs and requirements of customers and satisfying them in an effective manner.

Codes:

(a) Both Assertion (A) and Reason (R) are true and Reason (R) is the correct explanation of Assertion (A).

(b) Both Assertion (A) and Reason (R) are true and Reason (R) is not the correct explanation of Assertion (A).

(c) Assertion (A) is true but Reason (R) is False

(d) Assertion (A) is False but Reason (R) is true.

2. A company was marketing air purifiers which were very popular due to their quality and after sales services provided to the customers. The company was a leading company in the market and earning huge profits. Because of huge profits, the company ignored the after sales services. As a result, its relations with customers got spoiled and the image of the company was damaged in the public. The top management became concerned when the profits for the current quarter fell steeply. On analysis, it was revealed that ignoring the after sales services was its reason. Therefore, the company took all possible measures to protect and promote its favourable image in the eyes of the public. As a result, the goodwill of the company improved in the society. Name and state the communication tool used by the marketer in the above case to improve its image.

(a) Add to cost

(b) Public relations

(c) Corporate communication

(d) Personal selling

3. State which of the following statement is true

   Statement I: Advertising lacks direct feedback.

   Statement II: Personal selling is highly flexible as the message can be adjusted.

   Choose the correct option:

   (a) Statement I is correct and II is wrong.

   (b) Statement II is correct and I is wrong.

   (c) Both the statements are correct.

   (d) Both the statements are incorrect.

4. 'VAY' Products Ltd. is a natural and ethical beauty brand famous for offering organic beauty products for men and women. The company uses plant-based materials for its products and is the No.1 beauty brand in the country. It not only satisfies its customers but also believes in the overall protection of the planet.

   Identify the marketing management philosophy being followed by 'VAY Product Ltd'.

   (a) The Production Concept

   (b) The Product Concept

   (c) Marketing concept

   (d) Societal Marketing Concept

5. __________ are culturally defined objects that are potential satisfiers of needs.

   (a) Needs   (b) Market offering

   (c) Wants   (d) Customers

6. __________ refers to the process through which two or more parties come together to obtain the desired product or service from someone offering the same by giving something in return.

   (a) Customer value   (b) Exchange

   (c) Mechanism   (d) Marketing

7. In order to promote the sales of the company, Mukund Limited has decided to offer consumer durable products at 0% finance. Identify the type of marketing factor being described in the above line.

   (a) Controllable factor   (b) Non-controllable factor

   (c) Environmental factor   (d) None of the above

8. Udyog, a car manufacturing company, has started its business with Zv-800 and slowly launched Zv-1000, Wagon-Z, Swy-fy etc. and offered various services like after sales services, availability of spare parts, etc. Identify the element of marketing mix referred here.

   (a) Product   (b) Place

   (c) Selling   (d) Promotion

9. A brand or part of a brand that is given legal protection is called __________ .

   (a) Brand name   (b) Brand mark

   (c) Trade mark   (d) Promotion

10. __________ refers to additional layers of protection that are kept till the product is ready for use.

    (a) Secondary packaging

    (b) Primary packaging

    (c) Packaging

    (d) Brand name

11. __________ includes the cost of producing, distributing and selling the product.

    (a) Product cost   (b) Demand

    (c) Pricing objectives   (d) Competition

Topic Test – II

1. In order to enhance the easy marketability of the products, Dev, a producer gets the home furnishing products manufactured in confirmation to the predetermined specifications. Identify the type of marketing function being described in the given case.

   (a) Physical distribution

   (b) Standardisation and grading

   (c) Transportation

   (d) Warehousing

2. **Assertion (A):** Advertising is perhaps the most commonly used tool of promotion.

   Reasoning (R): Advertising helps in increasing sales and thereby reducing cost.

   Codes:

   (a) Both Assertion (A) and Reason (R) are true and Reason (R) is the correct explanation of Assertion (A).

   (b) Both Assertion (A) and Reason (R) are true and Reason (R) is not the correct explanation of Assertion (A).

   (c) Assertion (A) is true but Reason (R) is False.

   (d) Assertion (A) is False but Reason (R) is true.

3. Match the column :-

I.	Transport	A.	there is direct face-to-face communication
II.	Advertising	B.	is one of the major elements in the physical distribution of goods
III.	Personal selling	C.	Undermines Social Values

   Choose the correct option:

   (a) I-C, II–B, III-A   (b) I-B, II-C, III-A

   (c) II-B, III-C, I-A   (d) I-A, II-B, III-C

4. Anthony is engaged in the manufacturing of refrigerators. He surveyed the market and found that customers need a refrigerator with a separate provision of water cooler in it. He decided and launched the same refrigerator in the market. Identify and explain the marketing philosophy involved.

(a) Societal concept   (b) Product concept

(c) Marketing concept   (d) Pricing concept

5. _________ refers to the act of storing and assorting products in order to create time utility in them.

(a) Warehousing   (b) Order processing

(c) Transportation   (d) None of the above

6. In order to get feedback about its new product launch, the company conducted an online survey through a short questionnaire. Identify the marketing function being mentioned in the given line.

(a) Gathering and analysing market information

(b) Marketing planning

(c) Product designing and development

(d) Packaging and labelling

7. Which of the following is/are the functions performed by a label

(a) Describe the Product and specify its contents

(b) Helps in Promotion of Products

(c) Grading of Products

(d) All of the above

8. Which one of the following promotion tools has mass reach?

(a) Advertising   (b) Personal selling

(c) Sales promotion   (d) Public relations

9. Mail order selling is a __ channel of distribution.

(a) Direct   (b) Indirect

(c) Direct and Indirect   (d) Sole

10. _________ involves designing and producing container or wrapper of the product.

(a) Marketing   (b) Selling

(c) Advertising   (d) Packaging

11. Royalty watch manufacturing company is a renowned company marketing watches. It performs various activities like, market analysis, product designing or merchandising, packaging, warehousing, branding, pricing, promotion and selling. The company maintains good customer relations through various follow up activities. This helps the company in procuring repeat sales orders. Name the concept related to the activities mentioned in the above paragraph.

(a) The Societal Marketing Concept

(b) The Selling Concept

(c) The Marketing Concept

(d) The product concept

Answers

1. (a)   **2.** (a)   **3.** (b)   **4.** (c)   **5.** (b)   **6.** (a)   **7.** (b)   **8.** (b)   **9.** (c)   **10.** (a)

11. (c)   **12.** (c)   **13.** (b)   **14.** (c)   **15.** (a)   **16.** (c)   **17.** (c)   **18.** (d)   **19.** (b)   **20.** (a)

21. (b)

Topic – I

1. (d)   **2.** (b)   **3.** (c)   **4.** (d)   **5.** (c)   **6.** (b)   **7.** (a)   **8.** (a)   **9.** (c)   **10.** (a)

11. (a)

Topic – II

1. (b)   **2.** (c)   **3.** (b)   **4.** (c)   **5.** (a)   **6.** (a)   **7.** (d)   **8.** (a)   **9.** (a)   **10.** (d)

11. (c)

CHAPTER 12

Consumer Protection

Summary

Consumer : Consumer is generally understood as a person who uses consumer goods or avails any service.

Consumer Protection: It means protecting consumer from the clutches of fraud producers or sellers.

Importance Of Consumer Protection:

From Consumers' point of view:-

(i) **Consumer Ignorance:** In the light of widespread ignorance of consumers about their rights and reliefs available to them, it becomes necessary to educate them about the same so as to achieve consumer awareness

(ii) **Unorganised Consumers:** Consumers need to be organised in the form of consumer organisations which would take care of their interests.

(iii) **Widespread Exploitation of Consumers:** Consumers might be exploited by unscrupulous, exploitative and unfair trade practices like defective and unsafe products, adulteration, false and misleading advertising, hoarding, black- marketing, etc. Consumers need protection against such malpractices of the sellers.

From the point of view of Business:-

1. **Long term Business Interest:** It is always in the interest of the business to keep its customer satisfied. Global competition could be won only after satisfying customers. Satisfied customers lead to repeat sales and thus helps in increasing customer base of the business.

2. **Business uses Resources of Society:** Every business uses the resources of the society and thus it is their responsibility to work in the society's interest.

3. **Social Responsibility:** A business has social responsibilities towards various groups like owners, workers, government, customers etc. Thus, customers should be provided with quality goods at reasonable prices.

4. **Moral Justification:** It is the moral duty of any business to act in favour of consumer's interest & avoid any form of exploitation & unfair trade practices like defective & unsafe products, adulteration, false and misleading advertising, hoardings, black marketing etc.

5. **Government Intervention:** If a business engages in any form of unfair trade practices then government takes action against it, which will adversely affect the goodwill of the company.

Who Can File a Complaint?

1. A consumer

2. Any registered consumer association

3. The Central Government or any State Government

4. One or more consumers, on behalf of numerous consumers having the interest

5. A legal heir or representative of a decreased consumer

Rights of Consumers

1. **Right to safety:** This rights includes concern for consumer's long term interest as well as for their present requirement

2. **Right to Information:** consumer has the right to get information about the quality, purity, standard & price of the goods or services so as to protect himself against the abusive & unfair practices.

3. **Right to choose:** means to choose an assurance of availability, ability & access to variety of products & services at competitive price.

4. **Right to be heard:** if a consumer is exploited then he has the right to be heard and be assured that his interest would receive due consideration.

5. **Right to seek redressal:** The consumer has the right to seek redressal against unfair trade practices or any other exploitation.

6. **Right to consumer education:** it is the right of the consumer to acquire knowledge & skills to be informed to customers.

7. **Right to basic needs:** every citizen has the right to fulfill the basic needs to survive & have dignified living. The basic needs include food, clothing, health, etc.

8. **Right to healthy environment:** the consumers have the right to be protected against environmental degradation.

Three Tier Judicial Machinery to Provide Protection to Consumers

1. District commission: District commission has a jurisdiction to entertain complaints where value of goods or services paid as consideration does not exceed one crore rupees. It consists of a President and two members, one of whom should be a woman, duly appointed by State Govt. On receiving the complaint, the district forum shall refer the complaint to the opposite party concerned and send the goods or sample for testing in a laboratory.

2. State commission: It is established by the respective state government and ordinarily function at the state capital. State Commission has a jurisdiction to entertain complaints where value of goods and services paid as consideration exceeds one crore but does not exceed ten crore rupees. If any of the parties are not satisfied by the order of State Commission can appeal against such order to the National Commission within a period of thirty days of such order.

3. National commission: The National Commission has territorial jurisdiction over the whole country. National Commission has a jurisdiction to entertain complaints where value of goods or services paid as consideration exceeds ten crores of rupees. If any of the parties are not satisfied by the order of National Commission can appeal against such order to the Supreme Court of India within a period of thirty days of such order.

Relief Available

- Remove defect in goods and deficiency in services.
- Replace defective goods with a new one with no defects
- Refund price paid
- Pay a reasonable amount of compensation for any loss or injury suffered.

- Pay punitive damages in appropriate circumstances.
- Discontinue unfair/restrictive trade practice
- Not to offer hazardous goods and services for sale

Consumer Responsibilities

1. Consumer must exercise his right
2. Consumer must be conscious
3. Filling complaints for the redressal of genuine
4. Consumer must be quality cautious grievances
5. Do not be carried away by advertisement
6. Insist on cash memo

Ways and Means of Consumer Protections

1. Self-regulations by business: Socially responsible firms follow ethical standards and practices in dealing with their customers Good and ethical practices encourage firms to realise that it is in their long-term interest to serve the customers in a rightful manner

2. Business association: FICCI and CII have laid down their code of conduct which lay down for their members the guidelines in their dealings with the customers

3. Consumer awareness: A well-informed consumer would be in a position to raise his voice against any unfair trade practices .

4. Consumer organisation: It plays an important role in educating consumers about their rights and providing protection to them.

5. Government: The government protects the interests of the consumers by enacting various protective measures

Role of Consumer organizations and NGO's

1. Educating the general public about consumer rights
2. Publishing periodical & other publications to educate consumers.
3. Providing legal assistance to consumers by providing legal advice etc.
4. Filing complaints in appropriate consumer courts on behalf of consumers.

Exercise

1. In which year did Consumer Protection Act come into existence?

   (a) 1991 (b) 1985

   (c) 1986 (d) 1990

2. Raj, a marketing manager is a patient of diabetes for which he takes medicines regularly. One day, on his tour to Patna, he met with an accident and was hospitalised. Due to doctor's negligence a delicate nerve of his right leg was cut rendering hum crippled throughout his life. Identify the consumer right that has been violated by the doctors under the Consumer Protection Act, 1986 in the above situation.

   (a) Right to safety (b) Right to information

   (c) Right to Choose (d) Right to seek Redressal

3. Which one of the following is not a consumer right?

   (a) Right to safety

   (b) Right to seek redressal

   (c) Right to be standardised

   (d) Right to be informed

4. (CERC), Ahmedabad stands for:

   (a) Consumer Education and Research Centre

   (b) Conservative encouraged and Research Centre

   (c) Customer education and report centre

   (d) None of the above

5. **Assertion (A):** 'Right to be Informed' is important for a safe and secure life.

   Reasoning (R): The consumer has a right to have complete information about the product he intends to buy.

   Codes:

   (a) Both Assertion (A) and Reason (R) are true and Reason (R) is the correct explanation of Assertion (A).

   (b) Both Assertion (A) and Reason (R) are true and Reason (R) is not the correct explanation of Assertion (A).

   (c) Assertion (A) is true but Reason (R) is False

   (d) Assertion (A) is False but Reason (R) is true

6. _____ right provides consumer a right to get relief in case the product or service falls short of his expectations.

   (a) Right to Safety

   (b) Right to be Heard

   (c) Right to seek Redressal

   (d) None of the above

7. **Assertion (A):** 'Right to be Informed' is important for a safe and secure life.

   Reasoning (R): According to this right, the consumer has a right to be protected against goods and services which are hazardous to life, health and property.

   Codes:

   (a) Both Assertion (A) and Reason (R) are true and Reason (R) is the correct explanation of Assertion (A).

   (b) Both Assertion (A) and Reason (R) are true and Reason (R) is not the correct explanation of Assertion (A).

   (c) Assertion (A) is true but Reason (R) is False.

   (d) Assertion (A) is False but Reason (R) is true.

8. A District Forum has jurisdiction to entertain a consumer complaint involving product value:

   (a) Up to Rs. 20 lakh

   (b) Up to Rs. 10 lakh

   (c) Between Rs. 20 lakh and Rs. 1 crore

   (d) Above Rs. 1 crore

9. A complaint can be filed against _________ who adopt(s) unfair trade practices.

   (a) Trader only

   (b) Manufacturer only

   (c) Trader and Manufacturer

   (d) Consumer

10. Which one of the following is not a reason for importance of consumer protection from the point of view of consumers?

    (a) Consumer ignorance

    (b) Consumer apathy

    (c) Consumer exploitation

    (d) Unorganised consumers

11. _________ mark is used for electrical products.

    (a) ISI (b) FPO

    (c) ISO (d) Agmark

12. Atul bought a packet of biscuit from a local shopkeeper and found that the ingredients given on the label were not legible. He complained about it to the company. The company sent a written apology stating that they will make sure that existing packets are withdrawn from the market and new packets with legible labels are soon made available. State the consumer right which Manuj exercised.

(a) Right to seek redressal

(b) Right to be heard

(c) Right to information

(d) None of the above

13. Assertion (A): According to Right to Choose, Marketers should not force the consumer to buy a particular brand.

   Reasoning (R): Every consumer has the right to choose from a variety of goods and services at competitive prices.

   Codes:

   (a) Both Assertion (A) and Reason (R) are true and Reason (R) is the correct explanation of Assertion (A).

   (b) Both Assertion (A) and Reason (R) are true and Reason (R) is not the correct explanation of Assertion (A).

   (c) Assertion (A) is true but Reason (R) is False.

   (d) Assertion (A) is False but Reason (R) is true.

14. Which of the following functions are carried out by the consumer organisations?

   (a) Publishing periodicals to impart knowledge about consumer issues.

   (b) Providing legal assistance to consumers.

   (c) Filing complaints in appropriate consumer courts on behalf of the consumers.

   (d) All of the above

15. _________ means any person who buys any goods for personal use.

   (a) Consumer   (b) Wholesaler

   (c) Trader   (d) Service provider

16. In case the consumer is not satisfied with the order passed in the state commission he can further make a appeal in the national commisision within the time period of

   (a) 20 days   (b) 15 days

   (c) 10 days   (d) 30 days

17. _________ is set up by central govt.

   (a) District forum

   (b) State commisiion

   (c) National commission

   (d) None of the above

18. Due to the negligence of the doctors, Aman passed away within a week's time after his surgery of the spine. Which of the following parties can not file a case in this regard?

(a) The consumer

(b) Any registered consumers' association

(c) A legal heir or representative of a deceased consumer

(d) All of the above

19. _________ is one of the redressal agencies for redressing consumer grievances.

   (a) COPRA

   (b) State Commission

   (c) Consumer Organisation

   (d) None of these

20. Don't , purchase in haste , this is an important of the consumer

   (a) Right   (b) Responsibility

   (c) Act   (d) All of the above

Topic Test – I

1. Rights of consumer are protected under _________.

   (a) Consumer protection 1986

   (b) Consumer protection 1990

   (c) Consumer protection 1982

   (d) Consumer protection 1991

2. The consumer has the right to get compensation against unfair trade practices under right to

   (a) Right to choose   (b) Right to seek redressal

   (c) Right to safety   (d) Right to safety

3. Which of the following are the ways and means of consumer protection?

   (a) Self-regulation by the business

   (b) Business associations

   (c) Government

   (d) All of the above

4. _______ is the standardized mark on jewellery

   (a) ISI   (b) FPO

   (c) Hallmark   (d) CERC

5. _______ are made to hear complaints of the value less than 5 lakhs.

   (a) Consumer forum at district level

   (b) State commission

   (c) National commission

   (d) None of the above

6. Which of the following is not an organization working for consumer protection?

   (a) Consumer VOICE

   (b) Consumer forum

   (c) The bureau of Indian standard

   (d) Consumer utility & trust society

7. Janta booked several rooms in a reputed five-star hotel in kerela for his destination wedding. On the day of his wedding, when his friend Ram, after attending the lunch party, returned to his room to take a shower, he had a fall in the bathroom. The bathroom was three stairs down to the bathing area and there was a handle bar to the right. On the second step, Rama slipped badly and fell on his face with a great force, resulting in multiple fractures. He filled a case against the hotel for compensation for the injuries suffered due to faulty designing of its room. Identify the right of consumers being violated in the given case.

   (a) Right to be heard
   (b) Right to seek redressal
   (c) Right to consumer education
   (d) Right to safety

8. On Sonia's birthday, her mother gave her a pair of gold earrings. After one month, Sonia observed that the earrings were losing their shine. She checked the mark on the earrings and found that it was not a proper Hallmark and her mother had been cheated by the shopkeeper. So, she filed a complaint in the District Forum which rejected it. Not satisfied by the decision of the district Forum, she was very much disturbed and after two months, she decided to appeal further. Can Sonia appeal against the decision of the district forum?

   (a) Yes, after 10 days   (b) No
   (c) Maybe   (d) Yes, after 20 days

9. Which of the following statements is not true with regard to the District Forum?

   (a) It consists of a President and three other members, one of whom should be a woman.
   (b) The members are appointed by the District Government.
   (c) A complaint can be made to the appropriate District Forum when the value of the goods or services in question, along with the compensation claimed, does not exceed ?10 lakhs.
   (d) All of the above

10. Which of the following activities lie within the scope of consumer protection?

   (a) Educating consumers about their rights and responsibilities.
   (b) Helping consumers in getting their grievances redressed.
   (c) Protecting the interests of consumers.
   (d) All of the above

Topic Test – II

1. Aisha had some problem walking on the road. she purchased a pair of shoes with high heels. After some time of using these shoes her pain increased as she did not know that there were medically recommended shoes available in the market for this problem. After a few days of giving herself rest she approached a shop where the medically recommended shoes were sold. she was amazed to learn that the company making the shoes was holding workshops at different places in order to make the people suffering with such problem aware of an available option. Which consumer responsibility was not fulfilled by Aisha?

   (a) Aware about various goods and services available in the market'.
   (b) Consumer must exercise his right
   (c) Consumer must be conscious
   (d) Filling complaints for the redressal of genuine grievances

2. When Aman, inspite of paying the full price of the plot in Haryana as per the terms and conditions of the allotment letter, was not given the possession of the plot by the builder, he filed a case in the State Commission. Identify the right of consumers being exercised in the given case.

   (a) Right to safety
   (b) Right to be heard
   (c) Right to seek redressal
   (d) Right to consumer education

3. **Assertion (A):** Many business firms have setup their own consumer service and grievance cells.

   Reasoning (R): Consumer has a right to get relief in case the product or service falls short of his expectations.

   Codes:

   (a) Both Assertion (A) and Reason (R) are true and Reason (R) is the correct explanation of Assertion (A).
   (b) Both Assertion (A) and Reason (R) are true and Reason (R) is not the correct explanation of Assertion (A).
   (c) Assertion (A) is true but Reason (R) is False.
   (d) Assertion (A) is False but Reason (R) is true.

4. A popular nationalised bank has been fined Rs. 5 lakh by the country's highest consumer court, National Consumer Disputes Redressal Commission (NCDRC), for not sharing complete insurance policy details with a customer. The bank has been ordered to pay the full amount as compensation to the customer. Identify the right of consumers being violated in the given case.

(a) Right to be heard   (b) Right to seek redressal

(c) Right to information   (d) None of the above

5. Right to _________ is a right to be protected against products which are hazardous to life or health.

(a) Information   (b) Safety

(c) Seek Redressal   (d) Consumer Education

6. Raman went to a shop to purchase a jean. The shopkeeper offered him 3 designs for jean. Nitish asked him to show him the jean which was on display. The shopkeeper told him that he could not buy that jean and would have to choose from the options provided by him. Out of necessity and lack of time Nitish purchased a jean out of the jeans shown by the shopkeeper. He paid him cash and didn't take the cash memo. Later, when he wore the jean at home and was about to leave, he found there were marks on the jeans. He went to the shop the next day and asked for replacement. The shopkeeper bluntly denied that the jean was purchased from him. Which consumer right of Raman is violated here?

(a) Right to safety   (b) Right to choose

(c) Right to be informed (d) Right to seek redressal

7. Which of the following statements is not true with regard to the National Commission?

(a) It consists of a President and at least five other members, one of whom should be a woman.

(b) The members are appointed by the Central Government.

(c) A complaint can be made to the National Commission when the value of the goods or services in question, along with the compensation claimed, exceeds Rs. 1 crore.

(d) Where the aggrieved party was not satisfied with the order of the National Commission, the case can be taken to the Supreme Court of India

8. The minimum age limit for being a member of a district forum as per consumer protection act is

(a) 60   (b) 50

(c) 45   (d) 35

9. Identify the right of consumers being exhibited in the picture.

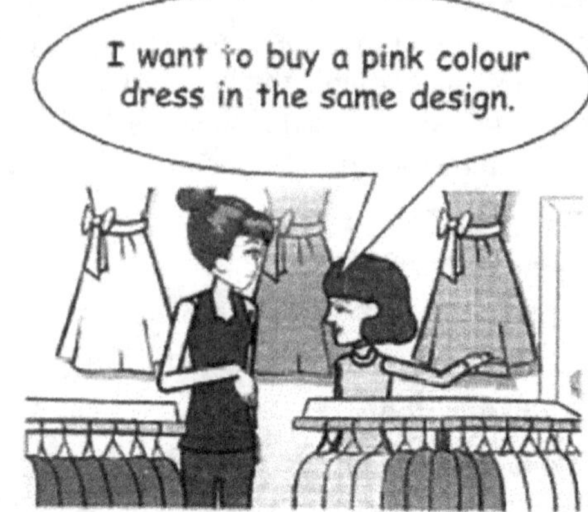

(a) Right to choose

(b) Right to be heard

(c) Right to seek redressal

(d) Right to consumer education

10. Robert bought a bottle of juice of a famous beverage company and found a glass floating inside the bottle. He forwarded a legal notice to the company, accusing it of the deficiency in service that could cause health hazard to the consumer. Identify the right of consumer being violated in the given case.

(a) Right to safety

(b) Right to be heard

(c) Right to seek redressal

(d) Right to consumer education

Answers

1. (c)	**2.** (a)	**3.** (c)	**4.** (a)	**5.** (a)	**6.** (c)	**7.** (d)	**8.** (a)	**9.** (c)	**10.** (b)
11. (a)	**12.** (b)	**13.** (a)	**14.** (d)	**15.** (a)	**16.** (d)	**17.** (a)	**18.** (a)	**19.** (b)	**20.** (b)

Topic – I

1. (a)	**2.** (b)	**3.** (d)	**4.** (c)	**5.** (a)	**6.** (c)	**7.** (d)	**8.** (b)	**9.** (d)	**10.** (d)

Topic – II

1. (a)	**2.** (b)	**3.** (b)	**4.** (c)	**5.** (b)	**6.** (a)	**7.** (a)	**8.** (d)	**9.** (a)	**10.** (a)

www.ingramcontent.com/pod-product-compliance
Lightning Source LLC
Chambersburg PA
CBHW081308130726

47998CB00010B/2973